Waiting with the Wildflowers

Jessica Cunningham

ZeeT Publishing

Table of Contents

Intro & Dedication

In this life, we walk through seasons of trials that refine us. I have found this to be true in my own journey, as I've faced many difficult seasons where it was hard to remember—let alone, imagine—the beauty waiting on the other side.

As a child, I endured abuse from people I trusted. As an adult, I faced similar pain in my first marriage. Through my divorce and the wilderness season that followed, I lost many friends and wrestled with deep feelings of abandonment and loneliness. It was a long, quiet season of waiting.

Yet, what I've learned in those hard places is something I wouldn't trade for the world. I discovered joy in the trials as I chose to cling to Christ rather than to my circumstances. I chose to wait and focus on the wildflowers that could *bloom*, instead of staring at what had *withered*.

As I sit down to write today, I find myself surrounded by a vibrant tapestry of wildflowers—each one a reminder of the unexpected blessings that have blossomed in my life. While I was waiting and trusting, God was quietly working behind the scenes, preparing the beauty that now fills my days.

I am now happily remarried to a truly exceptional man, blessed with a loving family, and honored to serve God through ministry. I am deeply grateful for the rich and varied experiences that have shaped me, and I embrace both the joys and the challenges because I know the beauty they produce.

I dedicate this book to Jesus, my first love, and to the beautiful family He has renewed and blessed me with—my husband, Forrest, and our three boys: Elijah, Enoch, and Jack.

Playlist for the Journey

Final Say
by Quay Worship

Anything is Possible
by Bethel Music

Jesus Did It
by Ramp Worship

Every Victory
by The Belonging Co

Believe For It
by CeCe Winans

You're Still God
by Philippa Hanna

Holy Ground by
Passion, Melodie Malone

I Won't Move
by Life Church Worship

Meet Me There
by Lydia Laird

No Turning Back
by Steffany Gretzinger

A Million Pieces
by Jessica Hitte

Whatever It Cost
by Rachel Morley

Make Room (Acoustic)
by Community Music

You Say/Who You Say I Am
by Caleb and Kelsey

How He Loves
by Abby Robertson

Sing Like the Battles Over
by Catherine Mullins

- Worship is the doorway where God steps close, reminding us that He hears every note and feels every tear.
- In worship, God doesn't just listen, He reveals Himself. Music becomes the place where His presence meets our honesty.
- Worship is where God whispers, "I'm here," and our souls finally exhale.
- In the middle of pain, worship becomes a lifeline, pulling us back into the goodness of God.

# Day 1: Look At The Lilies

"Look at the lilies and how they grow. They don't work or make their clothing, yet Solomon, in all his glory, was not dressed as beautifully as they are. And if God cares so wonderfully for flowers that are here today and thrown into the fire tomorrow, He will certainly care for you. Why do you have so little faith? And don't be concerned about what to eat and what to drink. Don't worry about such things. These things dominate the thoughts of unbelievers all over the world, but your Father already knows your needs. Seek the Kingdom of God above all else, and He will give you everything you need."   - Luke 12:27–31

This passage reminds us that God cares deeply—even for what seems small or insignificant, like wildflowers. It leaves us with one simple question: If He cares for the lilies, wouldn't He care even more for His people? The answer is a resounding *Yes*. Scripture affirms it again and again:

- God cares for you—1 Peter 5:7
- God is with you and will not leave you—Deuteronomy 31:8
- God loves you—1 John 4:9–10
- God knows you—Nahum 1:7

These verses, along with countless others, illuminate the truth of God's heart toward us. When Jesus points to the lilies, He isn't just admiring flowers, He is drawing a comparison to His beloved children. Lilies reflect breathtaking beauty, radiant purity, steadfast virtue, and the promise of new beginnings. What a powerful picture of the grace and salvation we receive when we choose to walk with Jesus, acknowledge our need for a Savior, and embrace the gift of a fresh start.

As we begin this devotional, I want to offer you a moment to connect—or reconnect—with Jesus. Whether you've never invited Him into your heart or you simply need a fresh breath of His presence, this is your moment. He cherishes you more than all of Creation, and He crafted the beauty of lilies for your delight.

He desires for you to rest in the fullness of true freedom found in Him. It is a purity that washes away the stains of the past, a righteousness that restores your standing with God, and a transformation that renews everything you thought you knew. Life may not always be easy, but when we walk hand-in-hand with God, the beauty and blessing far outweigh the burdens. Jesus gently lifts us from the weight of this world and invites us to experience the splendor of His kingdom here and now.

So, consider the lilies. Look at how deeply God cares for them. Then ask yourself, "Will you open your heart to Jesus as Lord and Savior, and allow God to care for you?"

A prayer for the day

*J*esus, when I look at the lilies, I'm reminded of how gently and faithfully You care for all You've made. If You clothe the wildflowers with such beauty, then, surely, Your care for me runs even deeper. Teach my heart to rest in that truth. I bring You my worries— the ones I speak and the ones I keep hidden. Lift the weight from my shoulders and replace my fear with trust. Let Your peace settle over me and quiet every anxious thought. Thank You for knowing my needs before I ask, for staying beside me, for loving me with a love that never shifts. Wash me in Your grace and renew my heart with the promise of a fresh beginning. Shape my life to reflect Your beauty the way lilies reflect the sun. Jesus, I open my heart to You—whether for the first time or as a returning child. Be my Savior, my steady place of rest, and the One I seek above all else. Let my life bloom in Your presence, and let my faith grow without fear as I walk with You into the fullness of Your kingdom.

In Jesus' Name, Amen.

Your Notes

# Day 2: Mud & Mercy

"I have told you these things, so that in Me you may have [perfect] peace. In the world you have tribulation and distress and suffering, but be courageous [be confident, be undaunted, be filled with joy]; I have overcome the world." [My conquest is accomplished, My victory abiding.]"

- John 16:33

Like a lotus rising from the mud to become a beautiful flower, Scripture reminds us that, in this life, we will experience mud—moments where we feel covered by it, weighed down by it, or even completely submerged beneath it. We don't have to be afraid of naming the mud for what it is. This divorce, this stress, this anxiety, this depression—whatever your mud may be—does not make you less Christian; it simply reveals where God longs to meet you.

What matters is what we *do* with the mud. We rise by surrendering it at the feet of Jesus. We confront it honestly, allowing ourselves to feel what surfaces in the process, without letting those feelings take control. We choose vulnerability with God—talking with Him about what hurts—and we lean on trusted friends or leaders as the Holy Spirit guides us to grieve what needs to be grieved so we can step into new mercies.

When we acknowledge the mud and surrender it to God, His mercy begins to penetrate the soil of our lives. He enriches what once felt heavy and lifeless, preparing it to nourish new growth. And, in time, just like the lotus, we rise—transformed into something beautiful, rooted in grace, and strengthened by everything we've overcome.
The Bible supports this in the following scriptures:

- God meets us in the mud and lifts us out—Psalm 40:1-3
- Trials produce growth, not destruction—James 1:2-4
- God's strength is made perfect in our weakness—2 Corinthians 12:9
- We are renewed day by day, even in hardships—2 Corinthians 4:16-17

When we take these scriptures to heart and actually apply them to our daily lives, something powerful begins to happen. The mud we walk through—those seasons of heartbreak, stress, anxiety, loss, or confusion—no longer has the authority to keep us stuck in the same place. Instead, in the hands of God, that very mud becomes the soil He uses to strengthen us, stretch us, and grow us in ways we never imagined. His Word reminds us that He lifts us out of the mud, renews us day by day, restores what was lost, and brings beauty from what once felt broken. When we surrender our struggles to Him, the mud doesn't define us; it becomes the environment where His mercy works deeply beneath the surface, preparing us to rise into something stronger, steadier, and more beautiful than before.

A prayer for the day

Jesus, you promised that, in You, I would find peace, even in a world filled with trouble. Today, I hold onto that promise. You have already overcome everything that overwhelms me, and Your victory is my steady ground. I bring You the mud of my life—the stress, the heartbreak, the anxiety, the places where I feel stuck or weighed down. Thank You that this mud doesn't make me less loved or less Yours. It simply shows where You long to meet me and lift me. Give me courage to surrender what I cannot carry. Help me face what hurts with honesty, without letting fear or emotion take control. Surround me with Your presence and with people who help me walk toward healing. Let Your mercy work beneath the surface, turning heaviness into soil for new growth. Renew me day by day. Strengthen me where I am weak. Transform what feels broken into beauty. And, like the lotus rising from the mud, help me rise—rooted in grace, steady in faith, and confident in the truth that You have already overcome the world.

In Jesus' Name, Amen.

Your Notes

# Day 3: Patience Planted By His Hand

"Because you know that the testing of your faith produces patience. Let patience have its perfect work, that you may be mature and complete, lacking nothing."

- James 1:3-4

Patience is not the engine that drives us forward—it is the anchor that holds us steady. It's not the prayer of, "God, give me strength to push harder," but the quieter surrender of, "Lord, keep me still and safe in You." Patience is the spiritual posture that refuses to drift, even when life's waves rise higher than we expected.

Just as a boat anchor keeps a vessel from being carried away by the currents, patience keeps our souls grounded in God's presence. An anchor grips the ocean floor so the ship remains secure even when winds howl and waves crash. But an anchor only works if it is strong, dependable, and dropped at the right moment.

In the same way, patience only holds us steady when it is rooted in Someone unshakeable—Jesus Himself. Nature teaches this same truth. The Blazing Star wildflower survives harsh prairies, droughts, and violent storms because of its deep, resilient root system. Its roots reach far beneath the surface, anchoring it through seasons that would destroy weaker plants. It blooms tall and radiant not because life is easy, but because its roots have grown deep enough to endure what comes.

Patience works the same way in our faith. It grows roots beneath the surface—roots of trust, surrender, and quiet confidence in God's timing. Patience doesn't rush the process; it strengthens us within it. It forms the kind of spiritual depth that keeps us from being uprooted by fear, disappointment, or delay. Like the Blazing Star, patience ensures longevity, hardiness, and the ability to withstand every kind of weather. This is why Jesus must be our anchor. He is strong, solid, dependable, and present in every moment we need Him.

Scripture reminds us: "This hope is a strong and trustworthy anchor for our souls… Jesus has already gone in there for us."
—Hebrews 6:18–20

Jesus has gone before us. He has walked through storms. He has endured pain. He has faced loss. And He rose. He is victory—not just for Himself, but for us. Whatever we face, He has faced it, too. Whatever threatens to shake us, He has already overcome. When we trust Him as our anchor, the winds of life cannot sink us. We may feel the waves, but we will not be moved

Patience, then, is not passive. It is powerful. It is the Holy Spirit teaching us to rest, to trust, and to remain rooted in Christ. It is the quiet strength that keeps us steady until the storm passes and the bloom comes. With Jesus as our anchor and patience as our deep root, we don't just survive the storm; we grow through it.

Jesus, teach my heart to embrace the kind of patience Your Word speaks of—patience that anchors me, steadies me, and forms maturity within me. When my faith is tested, let it not drive me to strive harder, but to surrender more deeply. Keep me still and safe in You. Lord, when the waves rise and the winds howl, hold me fast. Let my soul be anchored in Your presence, unshaken by fear or disappointment. Strengthen the roots beneath the surface—roots of trust, surrender, and quiet confidence in Your timing. Make me like the Blazing Star, able to endure every season because my roots grow deep in You. Thank You for going before me, for facing storms I could never bear alone, and for rising in victory so I can stand secure. Remind me that whatever threatens to shake me has already been overcome by You. Let patience do its perfect work in me, shaping me into someone mature, complete, and lacking nothing.

Holy Spirit, teach me to rest instead of rush, to trust instead of fear, and to remain rooted in Christ until the storm passes and the bloom comes. With Jesus as my anchor and patience as my deep root, help me not only survive the storm, but grow through it.

In Jesus' Name, Amen.

Your Notes

Day 4: When We Wilt, He Sustains

"Keep watch and pray, so that you will not give in to temptation. For the spirit is willing, but the body is weak."   - Matthew 26:41

We like to imagine ourselves as strong, rooted, unshakeable wildflowers, but the truth is, left to ourselves, we are far more like the poppy—beautiful, yes. Full of potential, yes. But fragile. Easily shaken. Quick to wilt under pressure. A single gust of wind can scatter its petals. A sudden heat can make it collapse. Its beauty is dramatic, but its endurance is short.

And isn't that the human heart without God? Poppies look bold and bright, but they bruise easily. Their petals fall at the slightest touch. Their stems bend under the smallest weight. They flourish for a moment, then fade. In so many ways, that is us—especially when we're leaning on our own strength. Our flesh is weak, sometimes we miss things, we make mistakes. We react before we pray. We fall apart faster than we want to admit. Without God's strength, we are easily overwhelmed. And without His Spirit, we tend to react out of our flesh—easily becoming more fearful, impulsive, emotional, or discouraged. Even with God, in seasons of struggle, we sometimes forget our roots. We panic. We grasp for control. We slip back into old patterns instead of anchored faith. Not intentionally, not rebelliously… just humanly.

Like the poppy, we can be dramatic in our distress, quick to fall apart, quick to feel undone by the weight of life. Our petals scatter at the slightest storm. Our emotions flare. Our confidence wilts. Our strength evaporates. But God never shames us for this. He knows our frame. He remembers we are dust. He understands our fragility better than we do. And He invites us not to pretend we are stronger than we are, but to let Him be the strength we lack.

God once whispered to my heart, "What's in front of you isn't a mountain to be moved; you're just in a ditch I never intended you to be in." And isn't that what happens when we try to handle life on our own? That's when the digging begins. That's when we pick up the shovel. That's when we exhaust ourselves trying to fix, control, or carry what was never ours to manage.

When we do things our way, we are picking up a shovel instead of picking up the cross. Jesus said, "If anyone would come after Me, let him deny himself, take up his cross daily, and follow Me." —Luke 9:23

When our hands are full carrying the cross, we don't have the capacity to pick up the shovel.

The shovel represents:
- Self-effort
- Self-saving
- Self-fixing
- Digging ourselves deeper

The cross represents
- Surrender
- Trust
- Obedience
- Letting God lead

And yet, even if we have picked up the shovel… even if we are in the ditch… even if we dug it ourselves… His grace climbs in. His mercy lifts us out. His love refuses to leave us buried. Because the God who sees fragile poppies also gifted us to grow in deep-rooted faith. And the God who watches us dig ditches is the same God who helps pull us out with compassion and strength.

We can be fragile, yes, but we are held by a God who is not.

A prayer for the day

Lord, meet me in my poppy-fragile places. When my flesh is weak and my strength wilts, hold me steady in Your grace. Keep my hands on the cross instead of the shovel, and lift me from every ditch I've dug. Grow deep roots in me—patience, trust, and surrender—so I can stand in what You've planted, not what I've tried to build on my own. Thank You for being strong where I am not.

In Jesus' Name, Amen.

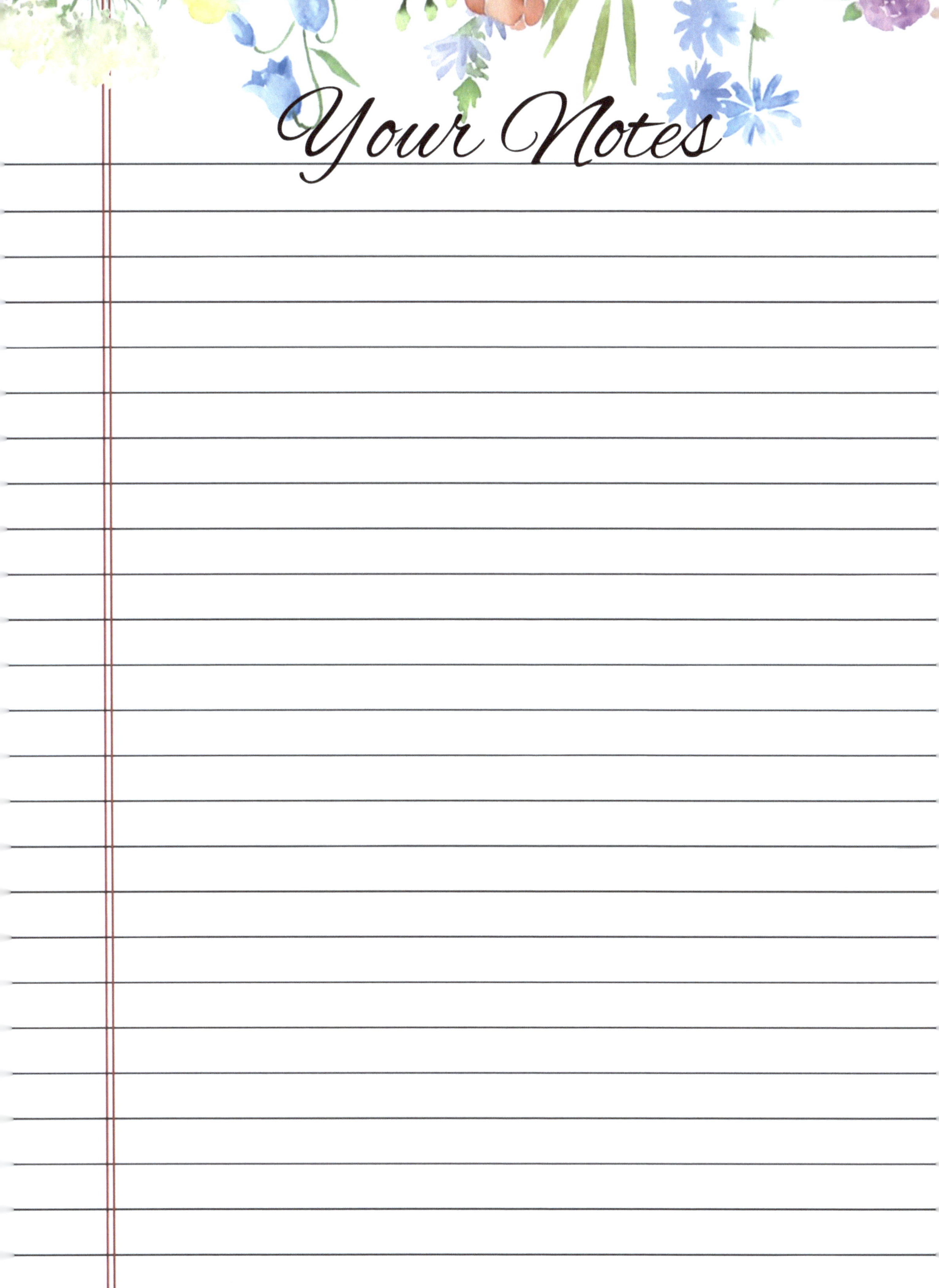

Your Notes

Day 5: Strength Found In His Likeness

"My dear children, I am writing this to you so that you will not sin. But if anyone does sin, we have an advocate who pleads our case before the Father. He is Jesus Christ, the one who is truly righteous. He Himself is the sacrifice that atones for our sins—and not only our sins, but the sins of all the world. And we can be sure that we know Him if we obey His commandments. If someone claims, "I know God," but doesn't obey God's commandments, that person is a liar and is not living in the truth. But those who obey God's Word truly show how completely they love Him. That is how we know we are living in Him. Those who say they live in God should live their lives as Jesus did."

- 1 John 2:1-6

Some orchids survive through mimicry. They imitate stronger, more attractive flowers—copying their colors, shapes, and even scents—to draw in the pollinators they need to live. On their own, they don't have the strength, beauty, or resources to thrive, so they imitate what is stronger.

And isn't that a picture of us? We were never meant to survive this life on our own strength. We were never designed to flourish by relying on our own wisdom, willpower, or goodness. Just like the orchid imitates a stronger flower to survive, we imitate Jesus to truly live.

This is exactly what 1 John 2:1–6 teaches—that those who claim to live in Him must walk as Jesus walked. Not perfectly, not instantly, but intentionally, maturing day by day into His likeness.

We are all on a journey of becoming more like Jesus, growing in our faith, and learning to surrender the parts of us which don't reflect Him. Maturity doesn't come from trying harder; it comes from surrendering more. It comes from being honest about the traits in us that don't look like Jesus and asking God to reshape them. Sometimes, it even means inviting trusted people into the process because transformation rarely happens in isolation.

Whatever it takes, the goal is simple: be like Jesus. And, yes, we will miss it at times. We will react out of our flesh. We will stumble, forget, or fall short. But that's why His grace and mercy run so deep. Grace doesn't excuse immaturity; it empowers growth. Mercy doesn't overlook our weakness; it lifts us from it.

To be like Jesus, we must know Jesus. Not through secondhand wisdom, not through someone else's revelation, not through impressive knowledge, but through a personal relationship. A daily walk. A surrendered heart. A love that grows deeper than anything else in our lives.

We have to love Him more than anything else. Because it's out of love—not duty—that we chase after Him. Not for a month, not for a year, but for a lifetime. The Bible wasn't given for our information; it was given for our transformation. Every page is meant to shape us, soften us, stretch us, and make us look more like Him.

A prayer for the day

Jesus, thank You for being my advocate—the One who covers my sin and leads me into truth. Your grace lifts me when I fall, and Your mercy invites me to grow. I surrender my heart to You again, asking You to shape me into Your likeness.

Lord, I know I cannot flourish on my own strength. Teach me to imitate You; to walk as You walked, love as You loved, and obey Your Word from a place of deep devotion. Show me the parts of my life that don't reflect You, and give me the courage to lay them down so You can transform them. Thank You that, when I stumble, You do not condemn me; You call me closer. Let Your grace empower maturity in me, and let Your truth take root in every part of my life. Draw me into a personal, daily relationship with You—one that changes how I think, live, and love. Make me more like You, Jesus. Day by day, shape my heart, steady my steps, and let my life reflect the One I follow.

In Jesus' Name, Amen.

Your Notes

Day 6: Fragrance Under Pressure

"Her hands are busy spinning thread, her fingers twisting fiber.
She extends a helping hand to the poor and opens her arms to the needy.
She has no fear of winter for her or her household for everyone has warm clothes.
She makes her own bedspreads. She dresses in fine linen and purple gowns.
Her husband is well known at the city gates where he sits with the other civic leaders.
She makes belted linen garments and sashes to sell to the merchants.
She is clothed with strength and dignity, and she laughs without fear of the future.
When she speaks, her words are wise, and she gives instructions with kindness.
She carefully watches everything in her household and suffers nothing from laziness.
Her children stand and bless her; her husband praises her:
"There are many virtuous and capable women in the world, but you surpass them all!"
Charm is deceptive, and beauty does not last; but a woman who fears the Lord will be greatly praised. Reward her for all she has done. Let her deeds publicly declare her praise."
                                                                                    - Proverbs 31: 19-31

A Proverbs 31 woman is often pictured as flawless—perfectly disciplined, endlessly capable, and effortlessly noble. For years, that passage felt unreachable to me. No matter how hard I tried, the standard seemed impossible. I read it as a checklist of perfection instead of a portrait of a woman strengthened by God. I didn't realize it wasn't about performing strength; it was about receiving it. It wasn't about being in control; it was about having power under control. That's when lavender came to mind.

Lavender is a quiet kind of strong. It thrives where other plants struggle—dry soil, rocky ground, harsh sun. The rough winds that bend it don't break it; they make its stems sturdier. And when lavender is pressed, crushed, or brushed against, it releases more fragrance, not less.

That is the strength of a Proverbs 31 woman. With God, she thrives in places others might wither. The winds of life don't destroy her; they deepen her roots. Pressure doesn't silence her faith; it releases the fragrance of it. Her strength isn't loud; it's steady. Her beauty isn't fragile; it's resilient. Her power isn't forceful; it's surrendered.

Also, I love purple, so while studying the Proverbs 31 woman, that detail jumped out at me. Does this mean I should wear more purple?

Not exactly. Purple in Scripture symbolizes wisdom, dignity, devotion, peace, creativity, royalty, and strength. It's not about the color; it's about the posture. As daughters of the King, we are meant to reflect the attributes of purple.

If we don't see those traits in ourselves yet, we should not shame ourselves—we spin them into our lives the way she spun wool and flax.

"She finds wool and flax and busily spins it." - Proverbs 31:13

Let God's Word be your wool and flax. Spin it into your spirit daily. Let it shape your posture, your strength, your identity. Let it weave wisdom, dignity, and devotion into the fabric of who you are. And live—always—in your purple gown. And, like lavender, be calm and strong.

A prayer for the day

Lord, thank You for the Proverbs 31 woman—not as a picture of perfection, but as a woman strengthened by You. Teach me to receive that same strength. Help me walk in quiet confidence, steady dignity, and a heart surrendered to Your wisdom. Make my spirit like lavender—able to thrive in hard places, able to stand in harsh winds without breaking, and able to release the fragrance of faith when pressed. Let my strength be steady, my beauty resilient, and my character rooted in You.

Clothe me in the true purple of Scripture—wisdom, devotion, peace, creativity, and holy strength. Where these traits are missing, help me weave them into my life through Your Word. Shape my posture, my identity, and my daily choices until they reflect the heart of a daughter of the King. Teach me to speak with kindness, serve with compassion, and watch over what You've entrusted to me with faithfulness. Let me laugh without fear of the future because my confidence is in You alone.

Lord, weave Your wisdom into me. Root Your strength within me and let my life reflect the beauty of a woman who walks closely with You—calm, strong, and clothed in purple.

In Jesus' Name, Amen.

Your Notes

Day 7: Uproot the Offense

"I also pray that you will understand the incredible greatness of God's power for us who believe him. This is the same mighty power that raised Christ from the dead and seated him in the place of honor at God's right hand in the heavenly realms. Now he is far above any ruler or authority or power or leader or anything else—not only in this world but also in the world to come. God has put all things under the authority of Christ and has made Him head over all things for the benefit of the church. And the church is His body; it is made full and complete by Christ, who fills all things everywhere with Himself."

- Ephesians 1:19-23

Periwinkle is a small, pretty flower with soft purple petals and gentle vines—a plant that looks harmless at first glance, but beneath its beauty lies a quiet danger. Periwinkle spreads aggressively, rooting itself in every open space, choking out native wildflowers, stealing their light, water, leaving them no room to grow. What begins as something small can take over an entire garden if left unchecked.

Church hurt can feel the same. Sometimes, the wound comes from intentional harm; sometimes, it comes from accidents, misunderstandings, immaturity, or leaders who were supposed to protect but didn't. Either way, the pain is real. And, like periwinkle, if left alone, it can spread—quietly, deeply, and aggressively.

- Offense can take root in the hidden places of the heart.
- Bitterness can creep along the edges of our thoughts.
- Distrust can smother the tender places where faith once bloomed.

What started as one painful moment can begin to take over everything. But here's the truth: God doesn't hurt people; people do. And, sometimes, the people who hurt us are the very ones who are supposed to lead us—pastors, leaders, mentors… vessels chosen by God, yes, but still human. Still flesh. Still capable of failure. It's important for us to remember the real pastor of the church has always been and is the Holy Spirit. We show up to experience God's Spirit working through man.

We honor the vessels God uses, but we must never forget that the vessel is not the source. And because the vessel is human, we must pray, forgive, and show grace, mercy, and love—even when it's hard. God will always deal with the faults of any leader who is submitted to Him.

So, let the offense go. Give it to God. Pull up the roots before they spread like periwinkle and poison your spirit. Heal, and return to Church—not for man, but for God. Because we don't gather to hear a man or woman preach; we gather to hear the Holy Spirit. We gather to meet with Jesus. We gather because the Church is His body, and He is the head over all things.

If you trust God to correct His people, then you don't have to hold on to the offense they caused.

- Do you trust that God will correct them if needed?
- Do you trust that He is the supreme authority over His church?
- Do you trust that He can take what was meant for evil and turn it for good?

Healing from Church hurt is hard—but it is holy. And it *is* necessary. Let God restore what was broken. Let Him replant what was uprooted. Let Him heal what was wounded. Let God be God. Let Him handle the hurt. Let Him judge rightly and heal deeply. Your job is to love Him, love yourself, and find joy again in your salvation. And, if you've walked away, all it takes is one simple, "Lord, I'm sorry."

God loves you so much. Never forget that.

Jesus, thank You for the power You've given to those who believe—the same power that raised You from the dead and placed You above every authority. You are the head of the Church, the One who fills all things, and the One who heals what has been broken. I bring You every wound, every disappointment, and every root of offense in my heart. Pull them up gently but completely. Cleanse the places where bitterness has grown, and restore the tender places where faith once bloomed. Help me trust Your authority over Your Church. Teach me to forgive, to release what hurt me, and to return to You—not for man, but for Your presence. Guard my heart from anything that tries to choke out Your light. Heal what was wounded. Restore what was lost. Make me whole again, and draw me back into joy, freedom, and fellowship with You.

In Jesus' Name, Amen.

Your Notes

Day 8: The Beauty Of Backward Growth

"Jesus answered, "My Kingdom is not an earthly kingdom. If it were, my followers would fight to keep me from being handed over to the Jewish leaders. But my Kingdom is not of this world."
                                                                                                              - John 18:36

Creeping bellflower doesn't grow like other flowers. While most plants push upward first—stretching toward the sun, racing to be seen—creeping bellflower grows down before it grows up. It sends its strength into the hidden places, building deep roots long before a single bloom appears.

To anyone watching from the surface, it looks like it's moving backward… like it's wasting time… like it's falling behind. But it isn't. It's *preparing*. And that's exactly how God grows us. The kingdom of God has never worked like the world around us. Everything about it is beautifully reversed:

- To receive, we give.
- To lead, we serve.
- To be first, we choose last.
- To find our life, we lay it down.

So, what if the seasons that feel slow, still, or even backward are actually the seasons where God is doing His deepest work? What if the moments where we feel unseen are the moments where He sees us most clearly? What if the times we feel lost are the times we are actually being rooted?

Because when we move "backward" from the world's perspective—away from striving, away from self-promotion, away from comfort and control—we are often moving forward with God. Closer to His heart. Closer to His will. Closer to the person He is shaping us to become.

Creeping bellflower teaches us that downward growth is not wasted growth. Hidden growth is not a lesser growth. Backward growth is not failure; it's foundation. Sometimes, God uses what takes us down before He brings us up. Sometimes, He slows us so He can steady us. Sometimes, He hides us so He can heal us. Sometimes, He pulls us away from what *looks like* progress to prepare us for what *is* progress.

What if the seasons that feel "backwards" aren't failures at all, but the very seasons were God shape us the most? What if digging down is the only way to rise up? What if God is transforming our minds to understand His Kingdom by first undoing everything the world taught us?

Maybe what feels like delay is really quiet development. Maybe the places that feel like loss God's turning into great gains. Maybe the places that feel backward are actually the very times God is moving us forward. In God's Kingdom, backward is often the beginning of a breakthrough.

A prayer for the day

Jesus, thank You for reminding me that Your Kingdom is not of this world. Teach my heart to live by Heaven's rhythms, not the world's expectations. When life feels slow, still, or even backward, help me trust that You are doing a deeper work beneath the surface.

Lord, grow my roots in the hidden places. Strengthen me in the quiet, unseen seasons. When I feel overlooked, remind me that You see me. When I feel lost, anchor me in the truth that You are rooting me more firmly in Your will. Help me embrace the beautiful reversals of Your Kingdom—giving instead of grasping, serving instead of striving, surrendering instead of controlling. Let downward growth become my foundation, not my fear. Let every delay become development, every setback become shaping, and every "backward" moment become preparation for breakthrough.

Steady me when You slow me. Heal me when You hide me. Prepare me when You pull me away from what looks like progress. Make me willing to grow down so that, in Your timing, I can rise up. Jesus, transform my mind, reshape my desires, and lead me into the kind of growth that lasts. In every season—forward or backward—draw me closer to Your heart.

In Jesus' Name, Amen.

Your Notes

Day 9: When Flowers Listen

"Don't use foul or abusive language. Let everything you say be good and helpful, so that your words will be an encouragement to those who hear them."

- Ephesians 4: 29

There's a well-known study showing that when people speak kindly to flowers, they grow stronger, fuller, and more vibrant. But when spoken to harshly, the flowers will weaken, wilt, or even die. Scientists call it sound vibration; Scripture calls it a reminder.

Because, if flowers respond to words, how much more do people? We grew up hearing, "Sticks and stones may break my bones, but words will never hurt me." But the truth is far more sobering: sticks and stones *can* break bones—and words *absolutely* have the power to hurt, destroy, build, or shape us.

Sometimes, what we're facing isn't spiritual warfare at all, but personal *wordfare*—the battle created by the very words we speak, repeat, or agree with. Proverbs 18:21 tells us plainly, "The tongue has the power of life and death." This wasn't poetic exaggeration; it was divine design."

God created the world with His words, then He created us in His image, with the ability to echo that same creative authority. Genesis 1:26–28 declares that we were made in His likeness and given dominion. He spoke, and Creation was manifested. We speak, and atmospheres shift. Our words build worlds. Our words plant seeds. Our words water or wither that which grows in our lives.

Because Scripture teaches that our words carry spiritual weight, it also teaches that there is an enemy who listens for what he can use against us. And while God is omniscient, the enemy is not. He only knows what he hears. So, when we speak fear, defeat, shame, or hopelessness, we hand him vocabulary to use against us.

- Church—be careful with your words.
- Do not claim what is not your portion.
- Do not label yourself with what God never named you.
- Do not water weeds with your confession.

Your portion is life in Christ. Your purpose is multiplication. Your identity is light. Scripture keeps circling back to this truth:

- 1 Peter 3:10: "Whoever desires to love life and see good days, let him keep his tongue from evil…"
- Ephesians 4:29: "Let no corrupting talk come out of your mouths, but only what is good for building up…"

God is not restricting us; He is protecting the garden of our lives—your words are seeds, your words are water, your words are climate, your words are atmosphere.

So, speak life. Speak promise. Speak Scripture. Speak identity. Speak destiny. Let your words water the seeds God planted. Let them nourish the flowers in your life. Let them strengthen what is blooming. Let them call forth what is still buried.

May your tongue become a wellspring of life, and may your world bloom under the sound of truth, kindness, and God-given authorship.

Lord, guard my mouth and shape my speech. Let every word I speak carry life, truth, and kindness. Uproot anything in me that tears down, and plant in me a heart that builds up. Teach me to speak with wisdom and grace, watering what You've planted, and refusing to agree with anything that is not from You. May my words become seeds of encouragement and may the atmosphere around me bloom under the sound of Your truth.

In Jesus' Name, Amen.

Your Notes

Day 10: Bloom Again

"And finally Saul son of Kish was chosen from among them. But when they looked for him, he had disappeared. So, they asked the Lord, "Where is he?" And the Lord replied, "He is hiding among the baggage." So, they found him and brought him out, and he stood head and shoulders above anyone else. Then Samuel said to all the people, "This is the man the Lord has chosen as your king. No one in all Israel is like him.' And all the people shouted, "Long live the king!"   - 1 Samuel 10: 21-24

The mayapple is a wildflower with a secret: its blossom doesn't appear above its leaves like most flowers. Instead, it blooms under the canopy, tucked beneath its umbrella-shaped foliage. You have to kneel down, look closely, and search intentionally to even see it. The flower is there—beautiful, delicate, purposeful—but hidden. Sometimes, we are the same.

There are seasons when life becomes heavy, when expectations feel crushing, when pain or pressure makes us want to fold inward. We hide our gifts, our beauty, our calling, our voice. Not because those things disappear, but because *we* disappear behind them. Like the mayapple, the bloom is still there… but hidden beneath the canopy of our own fear, insecurity, or exhaustion.

The Danger of Hiding

But here's the danger: if the mayapple stays hidden too long, its petals wilt. If it remains covered too long, parts of the plant become toxic. The same can happen to us. When we hide too long—behind pain, behind people's opinions, behind shame, behind expectations—the beauty God placed within us begins to wither. Our hearts can grow toxic with comparison, doubt, resentment, or fear. Hiddenness can protect for a moment, but it can also suffocate if we never come back into the light.

Scripture gives us a vivid picture of this in the life of Saul. When God called Saul to leadership, the weight of it overwhelmed him. Emotionally, he ran to hide… not behind a tree, not behind a wall, but in the baggage; the very place meant to hold the people's provisions became the place in which Saul tried to disappear.

Haven't we all done that? Hid behind the baggage of our past? Hid behind the weight of expectations? Hid because we felt unworthy of what God was calling us to? Saul wasn't hiding because he was rebellious; he was hiding because the weight of kingship felt too heavy. Israel asked for a king before it was God's timing, and Saul stepped into a role he hadn't felt prepared for.

Yet, even in that hiding, God showed him grace. God sent people to find him. God called him out by name. God reminded him of who he was:

"So they found him and brought him out… 'This is the man the Lord has chosen.'" —1 Samuel 10:23–24

God Calls Us Out

Saul hid, but God still called him. Saul doubted, but God still chose him. Saul felt small, but God still anointed him.

Maybe you feel like Saul today. Perhaps you've been hiding behind fear, behind pain, behind expectations, behind the weight of what you think you're not. If so, I pray God sends people to find you. People who will speak life over you. People who will remind you that you are enough, that you are called, that you are chosen, that you are not meant to stay hidden.

Don't despise your hiding season; sometimes, God uses it to birth humility, dependence, and a depth that can't be taught any other way. But don't stay there. Don't let shame convince you that hiding is safer than healing. Don't let fear keep you beneath the canopy when God is calling you to bloom in the open.

Hold onto peace. Hold onto God. Stand with humble confidence as a child of the King. You *are* enough—not because of your perfection, but because of Jesus, the One True King who has given you everything you need for the place where He's called you to stand.

Hiding may happen, but it is never God's intention for your story. Come out of the shadows. Step into the light of the Son. Let Jesus wash you clean, refresh your soul, and bring your beauty back into full bloom.

A prayer for the day

Jesus, call me out from beneath the canopy where fear and weariness have kept me hidden. Speak to the places in me that have grown quiet, and remind me that the beauty You planted within me is still alive, still waiting to bloom in Your light. Pull up every root of shame, doubt, and insecurity, and replace them with confidence, clarity, and grace.

Lead me back into the open spaces You've prepared for me. Give me the courage to stand in the place You've chosen, even when it feels unfamiliar or uncomfortable. Let Your presence draw me out of the shadows, steady my heart, and teach me to trust the way You see me. Help me bloom again—fully, freely, and fearlessly—in the warmth of Your love.

In Jesus' Name, Amen.

Your Notes

Day 11: Stand Tall

"And I am certain that God, who began the good work within you, will continue His work until it is finally finished on the day when Christ Jesus returns."

- Philippians 1:6

Black-eyed Susans are wildflowers that carry a quiet, unmistakable confidence. They don't force attention; they simply grow toward the light, stand tall in harsh places, and bloom with a boldness that feels almost prophetic. They teach us something about the kind of confidence God desires for His people.

These flowers grow toward the light, turning their faces to the sun. God calls us to do the same—to grow toward His Light, becoming closer to Him and letting His presence shape our direction.

"Being confident of this, that He who began a good work in you will carry it on to completion…"—Philippians 1:6

Black-eyed Susans have deep, anchoring roots, allowing them to withstand storms, drought, and rocky soil. God wants our faith to be rooted the same way—deep in His Word, steady in His truth, and unshaken by circumstances.

"Blessed is the one who trusts in the Lord… They will be like a tree planted by the water… it does not fear when heat comes."
—Jeremiah 17:7–8

They are often the first flowers to reclaim old territory, sprouting boldly in places that were once barren or broken. God calls us to reclaim territory, too—in our families, our communities, and our callings, yet not in our own strength, but in His authority.

Black-eyed Susans help their environment by spreading pollen that brings life to everything around them. God desires that we bring life wherever we go—encouragers, builders, and carriers of hope.

They stand tall in harsh environments, refusing to shrink back. God wants us to not only survive hard seasons, but to thrive in them, becoming testimonials of His sustaining power. And they multiply generously, scattering seeds that create more beauty than what was there to begin with. God calls us to multiply spiritually, to pour out what He's poured into us, to disciple, to encourage, and to give freely.

Confidence doesn't come from personality, perfection, or performance. Confidence comes when God speaks over you… and you believe Him. God gives you permission to step into what He's called you to do.

So, today, declare:

- My confidence doesn't come from personality, perfection, or performance. My confidence comes from God's voice — and I choose to believe Him.

- God has given me permission to step into what He has called me to. I will not shrink back. I will not disqualify myself.

- I will no longer hide what God wants to heal. I choose honesty. I choose vulnerability. I choose freedom.

- Vulnerability positions me for victory. When I open my heart to God, He strengthens me.

- Abiding in prayer breaks lies and builds truth. As I abide, my heart aligns with His will. As I abide, His voice becomes louder than my circumstances.

- Confidence is born in the prayer closet. Identity is formed face to face with God.

- When I take His yoke, I do more with less — because He carries the weight with me. His yoke makes heavy things light.

- Hurt people hurt people — but free people free people. As God frees me, I will freely give away what I've been given.

- I will scatter seeds of hope. I will spread the pollen of God's goodness. I will multiply beauty everywhere I go.

- I will stand tall like the Black Eyed Susan. I will grow toward the Light. I will root myself deeply in God's love. I will reclaim territory. I will thrive in harsh places. I will multiply generously.

- I am who God says I am — and I am called to bloom with confidence.

As you speak these declarations over your life, let them settle deep into the soil of your heart. God is not finished with you, and He is not distant from your story. He is tending you with care, watering what feels dry, and strengthening what feels fragile. Like the Black Eyed Susan standing tall in harsh places, may you rise with a quiet confidence — rooted, steady, and sure of who holds your life. Believe that every declaration you just spoke is true, and trust that God is growing something beautiful within you, something that will bloom in its perfect season.

A prayer for the day

Father, anchor my confidence in You alone. Grow me toward Your Light, deepen my roots in Your truth, and strengthen me to stand tall in every season. Call me out of hiding and into the fullness of who You say I am. Let Your voice be louder than my fear, Your presence steadier than my circumstances, and Your Spirit the source of my boldness. Make me a person who reclaims territory, multiplies Your goodness, and brings life to every place I stand. I say yes to Your calling, yes to Your healing, and yes to Your will.

In Jesus' Name, Amen.

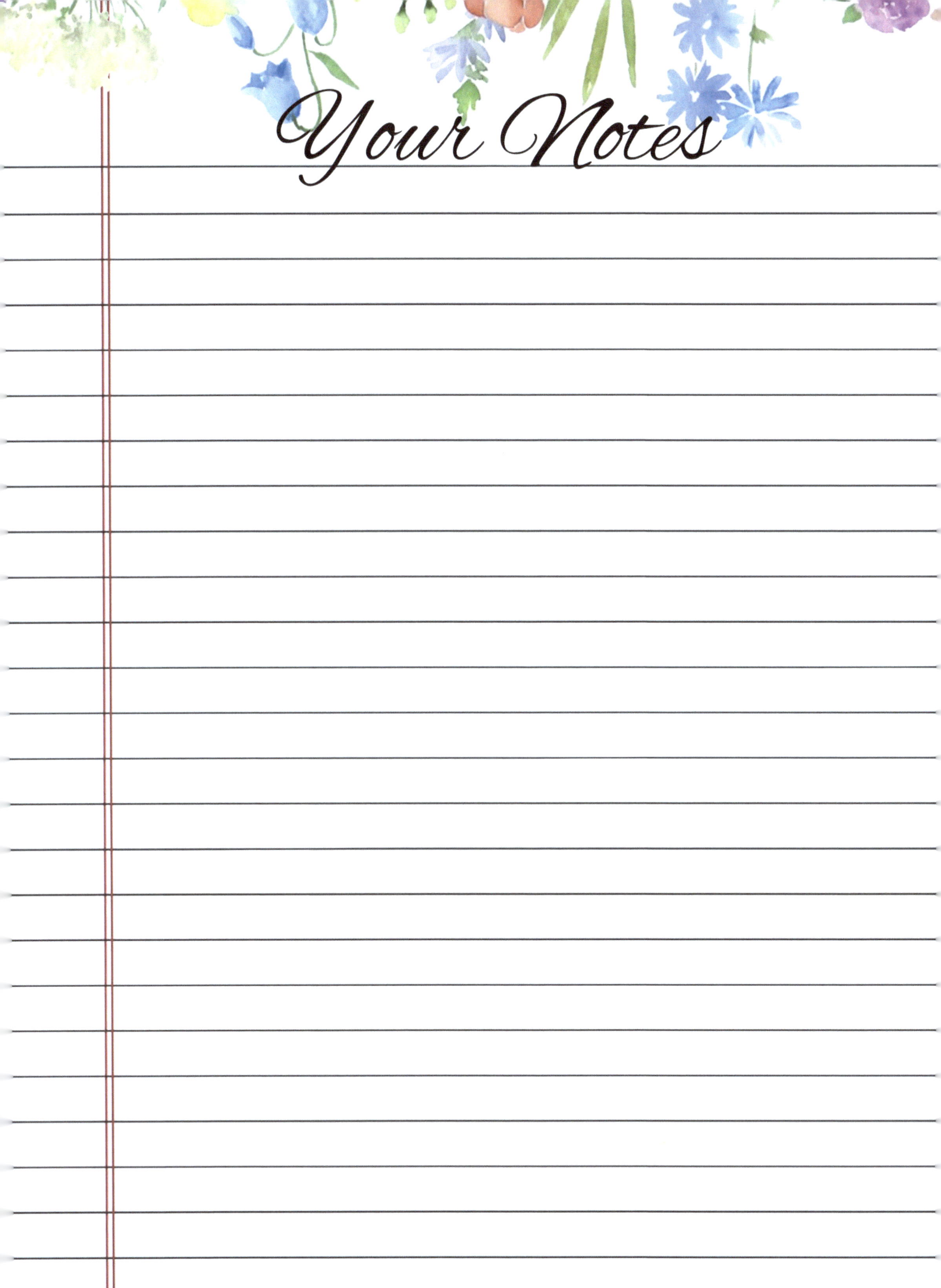

Your Notes

Day 12: The Heart Poured Out

"Meanwhile, Jesus was in Bethany at the home of Simon, a man who had previously had leprosy. While he was eating, a woman came in with a beautiful alabaster jar of expensive perfume and poured it over his head. The disciples were indignant when they saw this. "What a waste!" they said. "It could have been sold for a high price and the money given to the poor." But Jesus, aware of this, replied, "Why criticize this woman for doing such a good thing to me? You will always have the poor among you, but you will not always have me. She has poured this perfume on me to prepare my body for burial. I tell you the truth, wherever the Good News is preached throughout the world, this woman's deed will be remembered and discussed."

- Matthew 26:6-13

The bleeding heart flower is known for its tender, tear-shaped blooms—hearts that appear to drip with emotion. Each blossom hangs gently from an arching stem, telling a silent story of love, compassion, and vulnerability. It is a flower that weeps beautifully.

In Scripture, we see a woman whose heart wept in the same way. In Luke 7:36–50, a woman enters the room where Jesus is dining. She carries an alabaster jar of expensive perfume—the very best she owns. But what she brings to Jesus is far more than oil; she brings her heart, her tears, her glory, and her story.

Just like the bleeding heart, her tears told the truth of a heart that loved deeply. She knelt at Jesus' feet, broke open her perfume, letting her tears fall freely. John's account of this same moment (John 12:3) adds that she anointed His feet and wiped them with her hair. In that culture, a woman's hair was considered her glory—something to be covered, protected, and kept hidden. Yet, she uncovered it, lowered it, and used it to honor Him.

She didn't just give Jesus something valuable; she gave Him herself. Her act was wholehearted, selfless, and overflowing with devotion. Her tears were not shame; they were worship. Her vulnerability was not weakness; it was surrender. Her posture was not embarrassment; it was freedom. Like the bleeding heart, she bloomed in a moment of emotional honesty.

When she learned Jesus was at the table, she came with intention:

- Expectation to honor Him
- Preparation to give Him her best
- Devotion to pour out her love
- Surrender to lay down her glory
- Boldness to ignore the opinions of others

She didn't come to Jesus to get something; she came because she knew what she needed most was Him. She came to sit at His feet—fully exposed, fully surrendered, fully open.

Jesus received her offering with joy. He defended her. He honored her. He forgave her. He restored her. He set her free.

Her worship teaches us something vital:

- Do not come into God's presence guarded. Come vulnerable. Come honest. Come surrendered. Come with your heart on display.
- Don't come to church only to get what you need—come to give thanks for who He is.
- Don't raise your hands while keeping your heart closed—raise them as a sign of surrender.
- Don't hide your glory—lay it down at His feet so His Glory can shine through you.

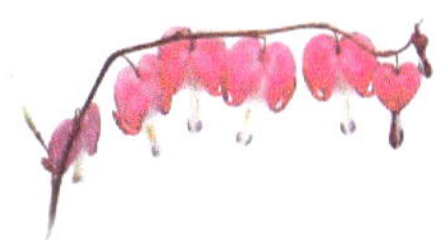

This woman's act was pure, humble, and overflowing with awe. Her faith was strengthened because her worship was sincere. We cannot represent His Glory while clinging to our own. We cannot walk in freedom while hiding our hearts..

Lay it all down. Pour it all out. Come fully exposed before your King. Love Him greatly. Serve Him wholeheartedly. And let your life—like the bleeding heart—tell the story of a heart that loves Jesus deeply

A prayer for the day

Lord, meet me in my surrender. Take my tears, my worship, and my whole heart, and let them rise to You as a fragrance of love.

Keep me humble, keep me close, and keep my motives pure. Shape my heart to honor You in all things, and let my love for You stay steady, sincere, and true.

In Jesus' Name, Amen.

Your Notes

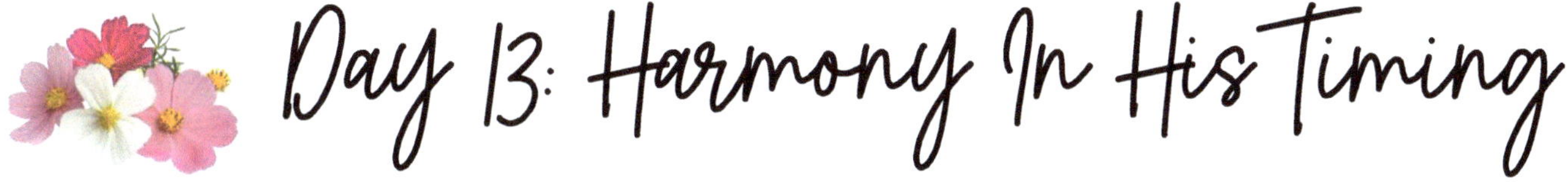

Day 13: Harmony In His Timing

"This was his eternal plan, which he carried out through Christ Jesus our Lord.

Because of Christ and our faith in Him, we can now come boldly and confidently into God's presence. So please don't lose heart because of my trials here. I am suffering for you, so you should feel honored."
                                                                                                    - Ephesians 3:11-13

The cosmos flower carries a name that feels almost prophetic: in Greek, κόσμος means "orderly world"—a world arranged with intention, harmony, and beauty, and isn't that exactly what God has done for us? He formed an ordered universe out of chaos, set time into motion, and placed us inside it as recipients of His goodness. Cosmos flourish easily, almost effortlessly. They grow in poor soil, bloom in long seasons, and stand tall with grace for which they don't need to strive. Their very existence whispers a truth we often forget:

Growth doesn't have to be hard when God is the One growing us.

The victory has already been won. Our redemption was purchased by the costliest gift the world has ever known—Jesus, His life surrendered, His death intentional, His resurrection powerful—all so we could live with purpose, freedom, and the indwelling strength of the Holy Spirit.

And as we grow, we discover another truth tucked inside His grace: Only with God do we truly flourish. Only with Him do we experience Eudaimonia.

The word Eudaimonia is a Greek term meaning flourishing; living the good life; possessing virtue, meaning, and deep well-being. The world chases this state endlessly, and because I assume you've lived both with God and without Him, I hope you've seen this truth, too.

Because He didn't just create an orderly world—He created an orderly plan to save us, free us, and bless us. Time, itself, becomes a gift when seen through this lens. We can't control it, but we *can* treasure it. We can't slow it, but we can fill it with meaning. We can't hold it, but we can honor it. God gives us time so we can:

- Love deeply
- Share the Gospel boldly
- Create memories
- Witness beauty

- Live fully
- Nurture our families tenderly
- Enjoy friendships
- Grow in Him

Every moment becomes sacred when gratitude opens our eyes.

Many people seek change, but you're discovering something richer—a deep anchoring in peace and gratefulness, knowing your next steps are guided by God's love. Thanksgiving becomes the soil where clarity blooms. Christ's redemption becomes the foundation where your future rests.

And, just like the cosmos—symbols of harmony, peace, and completeness—your life becomes a reflection of what happens when a heart is centered entirely on God. When we focus on who He is, when we remember how He has carried us, protected us, and proven Himself faithful in our testimonies, something beautiful happens:

We bloom. We flourish. We live settled, steady, and whole—not because life is easy, but because God is unchanging.

Cosmos remind us that peace is possible. Harmony is possible. Completeness is possible. Not through striving, but through surrender.

So, today, with a grateful heart, you can say:

Thank You, God. Thank You, Jesus. Thank You, Holy Spirit. For every gift, every protection, every moment, every breath. Everything is impossible without You, but, with You, all things flourish.

A prayer for the day

*L*ord, thank You for the gift of time and the order You've placed in my life. Help me flourish like the cosmos—at peace, centered on You, and growing with ease in Your Grace. Keep my heart grateful, my steps guided, and my life rooted in Your love.

In Jesus' Name, Amen.

Your Notes

Day 14: Made For Unity

"Abner shouted down to Joab, "Must we always be killing each other? Don't you realize that bitterness is the only result? When will you call off your men from chasing their Israelite brothers?"

   "Then Joab said, 'God only knows what would have happened if you hadn't spoken, for we would have chased you all night if necessary.' So, Joab blew the ram's horn, and his men stopped chasing the troops of Israel, nor did they fight anymore."

-    2 Samuel 2:26-28

Violets are astonishing when you look closely. With over five hundred species and a spectrum of colors—purple, white, yellow, blue—they reveal a world of diversity within a single family. And, yet, no matter how different they appear, they are all still violets.

Humanity mirrors this design. God created us with a beautiful complexity of diversity—different cultures, personalities, temperaments, gifts, and stories. Even though we are not the same, we share something profoundly human: we feel.

Our triggers may differ, but our emotions are universal: anger, sadness, joy, excitement, grief, loss, confusion, surprise, hope. We all know what it is to feel each and deeply.

And, yet, despite these shared experiences, we still manage to wound one another. We take offense into our hearts. We grow frustrated. We divide ourselves—even among friends, families, and, heartbreakingly, within the body of Christ.

But violets carry a message we desperately need. Across cultures, violets symbolize humility, modesty, repentance, and forgiveness—qualities God calls His people to embody. These are not optional virtues; they are the foundation of Christian unity.

Because loyalty must be our lifestyle, we cannot hold swords against our brothers and sisters and expect revival to occur. We cannot pursue Christ while refusing to pursue peace with one another. We cannot claim to love God while harboring hatred or resentment.

Scripture makes this painfully clear:

"If anyone says, 'I love God,' and hates his brother, he is a liar."—1 John 4:20

It's time to wake up. It's time to lay down our swords—the sharp words, the cold shoulders, the silent treatments, the assumptions, the gossip, the pride. It's time to confront issues with kindness, humility, and truth. It's time to pursue unity with the same passion we claim to pursue Jesus.

Because silence does not equal surrender. Ignoring conflict does not heal it. Avoidance does not produce unity.

We must speak. We must forgive. We must repent. We must reconcile. Offenses can become opportunities—for growth, for healing, for victory—if we choose humility over pride and unity over division.

It's time to blow the trumpet and stop justifying our offenses. It's time to surrender our swords at the altar. It's time to bear fruit worthy of repentance—with God and with each other.

When we stand together—in honesty, loyalty, humility, and forgiveness—our unity becomes a testimony. Our love becomes a witness. Our relationships become a reflection of God's Glory. Just like violets—diverse yet united—we were created to flourish together.

A prayer for the day

Jesus, soften my heart and teach me to walk in humility like the violet. Help me lay down every sword I've lifted against my brothers

and sisters, and replace offense with forgiveness, pride with repentance, and division with Your perfect peace. Make me loyal, honest, and courageous enough to pursue unity, speaking truth in love, and choosing reconciliation over silence. Grow in me a spirit that reflects Your heart—gentle, humble, and willing to forgive as I have been forgiven. Let my life bring You glory as I love others well.

In Jesus' Name, Amen.

Your Notes

Day 15: Blooming Without Defenses

"The Lord hears his people when they call to him for help. He rescues them from all their troubles. The Lord is close to the brokenhearted; he rescues those whose spirits are crushed. The righteous person faces many troubles, but the Lord comes to the rescue each time. For the Lord protects the bones of the righteous not one of them is broken!"

- Psalm 34:17-20

Roses are one of the most well-known flowers in the world—admired for their beauty, fragrance, and elegance. But roses also grow thorns—not because they are bad, but because they are trying to protect themselves in a harsh environment.

In many ways, God's people do the same. Spiritual abuse is tragically well-known in today's Church. It shouldn't be, but it is. The place that is meant to be a refuge, a home, a sanctuary of healing and truth, can sometimes become a place where people feel unsafe, unseen, or even harmed. And, when that happens, we develop thorns of our own:

- Thorns of self-protection
- Thorns of distrust
- Thorns of guardedness
- Thorns of silence
- Thorns of fear

But God never intended His house to be a place where His children needed defenses. Church isn't supposed to be comfortable, but it should always be safe. Just like roses, we sometimes grow thorns because of the environment in which we've been planted. But God does not want His people to live in constant defense mode—especially in His house. He wants us to bloom, not brace; to grow, not guard; to flourish, not fear.

Sometimes, when the soil becomes unhealthy, God will uproot us. Just as a gardener digs up a rosebush and transplants it to a place where it can thrive again, God may lead us out of a church that has become spiritually unsafe. Not because He wants us to run from discomfort, but because He wants us to grow in truth, maturity, and freedom.

But how we transition matters. If God is leading you to leave, staying out of fear, guilt, or pressure can turn you into a thorn—sharp, wounded, reactive. Thorns protect, but they also harm. In the church, we should never have to protect ourselves from the very people meant to shepherd us.

There is a deep need in today's Church for leaders who resemble the Father—leaders who comfort, correct with love, create safe spaces for hard conversations, and care for God's people with humility and gentleness.

If you don't feel safe, bring it before God:

- Why: Why do I feel this way? Why do I feel discomfort?
- What: What is the root issue? What steps should I take? What conversations should I have? What boundaries need to be set?
- Where: Where are You leading me? Where are you leading me to attend church? Where is my place in that community? Where is the environment that will help me grow?

God must always be the One we follow, above any pastor, leader, or church culture. We cannot let the failures or sins of others dictate our relationship with God or His Church.

I once heard someone say, "I've been hurt by shepherds and bitten by sheep, but I still love His Church." What a posture. What a declaration of maturity and loyalty to God's heart.

Sometimes, transplants are necessary for growth. Sometimes, staying is necessary for growth. But, in both cases, forgiveness is required. When God forgives you, your past is no longer part of your identity. And when you forgive others, their past can no longer be held against them.

Let it go. Drop the thorns. Follow the Holy Spirit's leading. Find the soil God has prepared for you. Forgive—fully, freely, and with the same grace you've received. Because God's people were made to bloom, not bleed.

A prayer for the day

Jesus, I come to You with an open and honest heart. Heal every place where thorns have grown in me from hurt, disappointment, or spiritual misuse. Uproot what is unhealthy, and plant me where Your presence is safe, life-giving, and true. Restore the places that have been trampled, till the soil of my soul, and breathe new life where hope has felt buried.

Give me discernment to know when to stay, courage to know when to leave, and humility to walk through every transition with grace. Guard my heart from bitterness, resentment, and self-protection, and teach me to forgive as You have forgiven me—fully, freely, and without keeping record.

Make Your Church a refuge again, a place where Your people can bloom without fear, where truth and love grow side-by-side, and where wounded hearts find safety in Your presence. Lead me by Your Spirit, anchor me in Your love, and keep my heart soft, surrendered, and responsive to You in every season.

In Jesus' Name, Amen.

Your Notes

Day 16: Stinky Alters

"Then he will sprinkle some of the blood of the sin offering against the sides of the altar, and the rest of the blood will be drained out at the base of the altar. This is an offering for sin."

- Leviticus 5:9

Skunk cabbage is one of the strangest wildflowers God ever created. It blooms early, melts snow with its own heat, and releases a smell that resembles rotting flesh. It's not pleasant, but it's purposeful. The stink attracts what is needed for the plant to grow, flourish, and fulfill its design.

In a strange, holy way, the altar of God has always carried a similar scent. In the Old Testament, the altar was never a place of perfume or performance; it was a place of sacrifice, a place where blood spilled, flesh burned, and the smell of death rose as an offering to God. Reading Leviticus makes this clear: offerings were orderly, instructed, holy, and set apart, but they also reeked. The altar was messy, bloody, and raw.

It was never meant to smell good. It was meant to smell like surrender. And even though Jesus became the final, perfect sacrifice, that doesn't mean the altar stopped being a place of "stink." It simply means the smell changed. It no longer held the odor of dead animals, but the odor of dead flesh—*our* flesh. Our attitudes. Our pride. Our addictions. Our habits. Our stubbornness. Our disobedience. These things stink, and they belong on the altar.

Scripture says,

"What is more pleasing to the Lord: your burnt offerings and sacrifices, or your obedience to His voice? Listen! Obedience is better than sacrifice and submission is better than offering the fat of rams." - 1 Samuel 15:22

Today, obedience is rare. Talk about obedience and you can almost smell the discomfort rise—stronger than skunk cabbage, stronger than death. People recoil, resist, or justify. But obedience has always been the fragrance God desires most.

That's why I believe our altars should be beautiful and stinky, just like skunk cabbage. Beautiful, because surrender is beautiful. Stinky, because dying to self, surrendering what doesn't look like Jesus, is never pretty.. The altar was never meant to be a stage. Never meant to be a platform for performance. Never meant to be a place where we pretend everything smells like roses.

The altar is where death happens so life can begin. Jesus laid His life down on the altar of the cross—the ultimate offering, the perfect sacrifice. His blood opened the way for us to pick up His cross, but He will never force us to carry it. We must *choose* to.

We must choose to be a living sacrifice. We must choose to let our lives become an offering. We must choose to lay down what stinks so we can walk out cleaner than when we walked in.

So, the question becomes:

What needs to die on the altar today? What attitude? What habit? What secret? What pride? What fear? What flesh?

When we lay down what stinks, God breathes life into what remains. And, like skunk cabbage pushing through frozen ground, melting snow with its own heat and blooming in the cold, we, too, can rise, flourish, and grow in places we never thought possible. But only *after* the altar. Only after the surrender. Only after the stink.

A prayer for the day

Lord, I come to Your altar with honesty and reverence, bringing the parts of me I would rather hide. Take every attitude, habit, fear, and piece of flesh that has begun to stink in my soul and lay it to rest under Your mercy. I don't want to carry what You're calling me to crucify. Teach me to choose obedience over performance and surrender over pretending. Strip away the pride that keeps me from bowing low and the shame that keeps me from coming close. Let this altar be the place where my old self dies and Your life rises within me. Make me a living sacrifice—willing, yielded, and ready to walk in the freedom that follows obedience. Lord, cleanse me, steady me, and shape me. As I lay down what stinks, let Your Spirit awaken what is holy, pure, and new.

In Jesus' Name, Amen.

Your Notes

Day 17: Faith That Reaches

"And a woman was there who had been subject to bleeding for twelve years. She had suffered a great deal under the care of many doctors and had spent all she had, yet instead of getting better she grew worse. When she heard about Jesus, she came up behind Him in the crowd and touched His cloak, because she thought, "*If I just touch His clothes, I will be healed.*" Immediately her bleeding stopped and she felt in her body that she was freed from her suffering. At once Jesus realized that power had gone out from Him. He turned around in the crowd and asked, 'Who touched my clothes?'

"You see the people crowding against you," his disciples answered, "and yet you can ask 'Who touched me?' But Jesus kept looking around to see who had done it. Then the woman, knowing what had happened to her, came and fell at his feet and, trembling with fear, told him the whole truth. He said to her, 'Daughter, your faith has healed you. Go in peace and be freed from your suffering.'"

- Mark 5: 25-34

Sweet peas are wildflowers with a quiet secret: they cannot grow upward unless they touch something. Their tendrils reach, stretch, and cling to whatever is near, and the more they reach out, the stronger they become. This is exactly what the woman with the issue of blood did. She reached, stretched, and pressed through the crowd with nothing but desperation and faith. With one trembling touch of Jesus' garment, she received healing. Just like the sweet pea, she grew stronger the moment she reached for Him. She wasn't just touching fabric; she was touching His victory. Every healing He ever released, every freedom He ever purchased, every battle He ever won… all of it flowed into her with one touch. Her desperation didn't push Him away; it drew her into the nearness of His arms.

In the Old Testament, the length of a king's robe represented his victories. When a king defeated another king, he cut off a piece of the defeated king's robe and sewed it onto his own. The longer the robe, the greater the victories. So, when Scripture says, "I saw the Lord… and the train of His robe filled the temple" (Isaiah 6:1), it is declaring something breathtaking: Jesus is the undefeated King. His victories are endless. His robe is immeasurable. And, now, *we* are the temple. This means the same victory that filled the woman when she touched Him is the same victory that fills us today. Every triumph Christ has won resides in us because His Spirit dwells in us.

A sweet pea symbolizes blissfulness, relief, and joyful release, the very emotions the woman must have felt when healing surged through her body. Just like the sweet pea, she reached out, touched what she needed, grew stronger because of the connection, refused to let anything block her path, and pressed through the crowd with boldness and faith. We can do the same. When we reach toward Jesus, when we cling to Him, lean on Him, and stretch toward His presence, we grow upward. We grow stronger. We grow freer. Touching Jesus is touching victory.

Sweet peas don't grow by standing still; they grow by reaching. So do we. The woman didn't wait for Jesus to come to her; she moved toward Him. She pushed past obstacles, opinions, and limitations because she knew one truth: if she could just touch Him, everything would change.

And it did.

Her story invites us to do the same—to reach again, to stretch again, to cling again, to press through whatever crowds our hearts and touch the One whose robe fills the temple. His victory is already ours. His virtue is already flowing. His presence is already near. We just have to reach.

Jesus, teach me to reach for You the way the sweet pea reaches for what helps it grow. Give me the courage to press past every obstacle and lay hold of the hem of Your garment with faith. When I reach for You, let me touch Your victory—Your healing, Your freedom, Your strength.

You are the undefeated King whose robe fills the temple, and because Your Spirit lives in me, your triumph fills me, too. Help me cling to You, lean on You, and grow upward in Your presence. When my heart feels crowded or weary, stir me to stretch toward You again.

Your nearness is my strength. Your victory is my portion. Lord, help me reach.

In Jesus' Name, Amen.

Your Notes

Day 18: Tables That Must Go

"On reaching Jerusalem, Jesus entered the temple courts and began driving out those who were buying and selling there. He overturned the tables of the money-changers and the benches of those selling doves and would not allow anyone to carry merchandise through the temple courts. And as he taught them, he said, "Is it not written, '*My house will be called a house of prayer for all nations*? But you have made it *a den of robbers.* The chief priests and the teachers of the law heard this and began looking for a way to kill him, for they feared him, because the whole crowd was amazed at his teaching."   - Mark 11:15-18

Most people hear the story of Jesus flipping tables and imagine a moment of explosive anger. But righteous anger is never reckless; it's restorative. It's protective. It's purposeful. When you look closely, Jesus' actions in the temple, they mirror the nature of yarrow—a wildflower known as a master of restoration.

Yarrow is one of the first plants to move into damaged soil. It stabilizes what's been disturbed, strengthens what's been weakened, and prepares the ground for life again. In the same way, when Jesus walked into the temple and saw corruption, exploitation, and disrespect, He wasn't reacting out of irritation; He was stepping into a place that had been spiritually depleted and saying, "This ground belongs to My Father. This space was meant for holiness. I'm restoring what sin has damaged." Just like yarrow, Jesus moves toward what's broken, not away from it.

Yarrow is also a cleansing plant. It absorbs toxins from the soil, pulling out what contaminates, and purifying what's been polluted. Jesus did the same in the temple. His flipping of tables wasn't chaos; it was cleansing. It was a temporary clearing of corruption until He Himself would become the permanent solution to sin's stain. Yarrow cleanses soil; Jesus cleanses souls.

"And now, because of His sacrifice, He doesn't just cleanse a building; He cleanses us, His temple." - 1 Corinthians 3:17

If we are now the dwelling place of the Holy Spirit, then the cleansing Jesus did in the temple is the cleansing He desires to do in our hearts. This is where the question becomes deeply personal:

Jesus, what tables do You need to flip in me to make more room for You?

Idolatry. Lust. Greed. Distraction. Misused time. Unforgiveness. Self-sabotage. Anything that crowds out His presence. Yarrow doesn't negotiate with toxins; it absorbs them. Jesus doesn't negotiate with sin; He removes it. But He won't force His way in. Your free will determines what He is allowed to take away.

This is why Scripture calls you to guard what God has entrusted:

- Guard your eyes (Matthew 6:22–23)
- Guard your heart (Proverbs 4:23)
- Guard the temple (1 Corinthians 3:17)

Don't become the thief of your own blessing. Don't sabotage the very things God is trying to grow in you. Don't let what Jesus wants to cleanse become what you cling to.

There is grace for every mistake, mercy for every misstep, and love strong enough to restore what's been damaged. But restoration begins with surrender.

Tell God today, "Lord, flip whatever tables in me need to be overturned. Remove what contaminates. Cleanse what distracts. Restore what's been damaged. Increase my capacity to do Your will Your way. Make me a temple that honors Your presence."

Lord, I come to You as Your temple. Just as Jesus cleansed the temple with righteous purpose, step into my heart and flip every table that doesn't honor You. Remove what contaminates, distracts, or competes with Your presence. Cleanse me the way yarrow cleanses the soil, pulling out every toxin and restoring what's been damaged. Guard my eyes with Your light. Guard my heart with Your truth. Guard my mind with Your peace. Increase my capacity to do Your will Your way. Make more room in me for You. Today, I surrender every table. Do Your cleansing work in me, Lord.

In Jesus' Name, Amen.

Your Notes

Day 19: Goodness In Every Season

"Rejoice in the Lord always [delight, take pleasure in Him]; again, I will say, rejoice! Let your gentle spirit [your graciousness, unselfishness, mercy, tolerance, and patience] be known to all people. The Lord is near. Do not be anxious or worried about anything, but in everything [every circumstance and situation] by prayer and petition with thanksgiving, continue to make your [specific] requests known to God. And the peace of God [that peace which reassures the heart, that peace] which transcends all understanding, [that peace which] stands guard over your hearts and your minds in Christ Jesus [is yours]."   - Philippians 4:4-7

When I look at the echinacea flower (also known as the coneflower)—strong, steady, and beautiful in every stage—I find myself in awe of the goodness of God. This wildflower mirrors His heart in ways that remind me just how deeply He loves, protects, and sustains His children.

Coneflowers survive the harshest droughts because their roots run deep. So do we—because God Himself is how we survive tough seasons. He is our strength when life feels dry, heavy, or uncertain.

"God is our refuge and strength, a very present help in trouble." - Psalm 46:1

The raised cone at the center of the flower is a fortress—spiky, guarded, and protected. It shields what's precious. God does the same with us. We are what is most special to Him, and He protects what belongs to Him.

"The Lord is faithful, and He will strengthen you and protect you from the evil one." - 2 Thessalonians 3:3

Coneflowers draw pollinators from every direction because what they carry is life-giving. In the same way, God draws good things to us. His favor attracts what aligns with His purpose.

"No good thing does He withhold from those who walk uprightly." - Psalm 84:11

One of the most beautiful truths about echinacea is this: it is stunning in every stage—seedling, bud, bloom, and seedhead. There is no "ugly phase." With God, there is beauty in the process of our lives, not just the outcome. He is present in the becoming, not just the blooming.

"He makes everything beautiful in its time." - Ecclesiastes 3:11

Even when the petals fade, the seedhead remains full of purpose—feeding birds, sustaining life, standing tall. God's impact on our lives never fades, even when seasons change. His goodness doesn't diminish. His presence doesn't withdraw.

"Jesus Christ is the same yesterday and today and forever." - Hebrews 13:8

Coneflowers are healing plants, used for centuries to restore the body. God heals us in the moments we need Him most. He restores what life has wounded, and strengthens what has weakened.

"He heals the brokenhearted and binds up their wounds." - Psalm 147:3

When echinacea drops its seeds, it multiplies quietly. One plant becomes many. God multiplies what we place in His hands. Nothing surrendered to Him stays small.

"Give, and it will be given to you… pressed down, shaken together, and running over." - Luke 6:38

Perhaps one of the most beautiful truths reflected in this flower is that coneflowers stand tall without competing. They don't choke out other plants; they simply flourish as they were created. In God's Kingdom, there is no competition between His children. He loves each of us fully, uniquely, and without comparison.

"See what great love the Father has lavished on us, that we should be called children of God." - 1 John 3:1

Because He loves us, He leads us. As I reflect on my life, I am in awe of God. The trials we face can transform us, reroute us, and draw us closer to His will. They lead us toward something more beautiful than we ever imagined, where new testimonies are birthed and past testimonies continue to reveal His Glory.

No shame, no trial, no struggle, no situation—NOTHING—can nullify God's Glory, goodness, or plans. Even when you can't see it, He is working. Even when you can't feel it, He is working. He never stops. He never stops working.

With God, there is purpose in every season. Praise God; He is so good.

A prayer for the day

Lord, when I look at the echinacea—strong, steady, and beautiful in every stage—I see Your goodness reflected in its design.

Thank You for being my refuge and strength, the One who sustains me through every dry, heavy, or uncertain season. Let my roots run deep in You.

Thank You for protecting what is precious, for surrounding me with Your faithfulness, and for drawing good things into my life according to Your purpose. Teach me to trust the beauty of the process—the seedling, the bud, the bloom, and even the fading petals—because You make everything beautiful in its time.

Heal what is wounded, restore what has weakened, and multiply what I place in Your hands. Keep my heart free from comparison, and help me flourish as You created me, confident in the love You lavish on Your children.

Lord, I stand in awe of how You lead, shape, and sustain me. Even when I cannot see or feel it, You are working. Your goodness never fades, and Your purpose fills every season of my life.

In Jesus' Name, Amen.

Your Notes

Day 20: Joy In Hidden Places

"In a little while you won't see me anymore. But a little while after that, you will see me again.

"Some of the disciples asked each other, *What does He mean when He says, in a little while you won't see me, but then you will see me,*' and '*I am going to the Father*'? And what does He mean by '*a little while*? We don't understand.

Jesus realized they wanted to ask Him about it, so He said, 'Are you asking yourselves what I meant? I said in a little while you won't see me, but a little while after that, you will see me again. I tell you the truth, you will weep and mourn over what is going to happen to me, but the world will rejoice. You will grieve, but your grief will suddenly turn to wonderful joy. It will be like a woman suffering the pains of labor. When her child is born, her anguish gives way to joy because she has brought a new baby into the world. So, you have sorrow now, but I will see you again; then you will rejoice, and no one can rob you of that joy. At that time, you won't need to ask me for anything. I tell you the truth, you will ask the Father directly, and He will grant your request because you use my name. You haven't done this before. Ask, using my name, and you will receive, and you will have abundant joy."

- John 16:16-24

Wild ginger is one of those wildflowers that teaches us something holy without ever raising its voice. It grows low, quiet, and unseen, yet it thrives. In its quiet thriving, it mirrors the kind of joy we have in Christ.

Wild ginger grows in deep shade, in places that feel dim or overlooked. So, too, can joy—because joy isn't dependent on sunshine, circumstances, or perfect seasons. Joy is rooted in Christ, not in what we feel.

Its flowers bloom beneath the leaves, hidden, tucked away where most people never look. Joy blooms like that, too, in the hidden places of the heart. In the moments no one sees. In the quiet corners of our lives where God whispers instead of shouts.

Wild ginger spreads slowly and steadily underground. It doesn't need to be loud to be powerful. Joy works the same way. It doesn't always burst in like laughter; sometimes, it grows like a steady warmth, a quiet strength, a gentle reminder that God is near.

Just like wild ginger attracts unexpected pollinators—beetles, ants—creatures most flowers ignore, joy can surprise us in places we never imagined: in grief, in waiting, in uncertainty, in the middle of storms we didn't ask for.

Joy isn't the same as happiness. Happiness rises and falls with circumstances, yet, joy is anchored in Christ.

Every morning, the sun comes up, and, every night, the sun goes down. Even when clouds hide it, even when storms cover it, even when you can't see it, the sun is still there, shining continuously. The same is true of joy.

Even when you don't feel happy, even when you're tired, overwhelmed, or hurting, joy is still present—steady, glowing, comforting. Never leaving. Never fading. Never dependent on how you feel.

Even when you cry, kick, or scream, joy is still somewhere close. Sometimes, all it takes is one deep breath, one moment of stillness, one reminder of what is good, pure, and true.

No matter what you're going through, no matter the storm, the sun is always somewhere, hanging around. So is joy.

Think on good things. Remember what is lovely. Hold close the people who love you. And, when life gives you a choice, choose joy. Choose it over fear. Choose it over sadness. Choose it over anger. Choose joy.

Just like wild ginger, joy can bloom in hidden places and unexpected seasons. It can rise up when happiness feels distant. It can surprise you in the dark. It can strengthen you when you feel weak. Why? Because joy is not something we manufacture. Joy is a fruit of the Holy Spirit, a gift from God, rooted in our salvation through Jesus. By His death, His resurrection. His victory.

So don't fight it when joy rises up unexpectedly. Press in. Lean into it. Ask God for more. And, on the days you don't feel joy at all, choose it—or simply ask God to help you find it. He will. Because joy, like wild ginger, is proof that God can make beautiful things grow even in the shadows

A prayer for the day

Jesus, thank You for the kind of joy that doesn't depend on sunshine or perfect seasons, but on You alone. Teach my heart to grow like wild ginger—low, quiet, unseen, yet deeply rooted in Your presence. Let joy take root in the hidden places of my soul, blooming beneath the surface even when life feels dim or overlooked.

When my days feel heavy, when storms hide the light, remind me that joy is still here—steady, warm, and close. Help me recognize the gentle ways You whisper to my heart, the quiet strength You place within me, and the unexpected moments where joy rises in places I never thought it could. Anchor me in the truth that joy is a fruit of Your Spirit, not something I have to manufacture. Let it grow slowly and steadily, spreading through every part of my life, a quiet reminder that You are near. When grief comes, when waiting stretches long, when uncertainty surrounds me, let joy surprise me with its presence. Teach me to choose joy—over fear, over sadness, over anger. And, on the days I cannot find it, help me ask for it. Help me breathe deeply, think on what is lovely, and hold close the people who love me. Make my life a testimony that You can grow beautiful things even in the shadows.

In Jesus' Name, Amen.

Your Notes

Day 21: Written In The Wild

"But you are not controlled by your sinful nature. You are controlled by the Spirit if you have the Spirit of God living in you. (And remember that those who do not have the Spirit of Christ living in them do not belong to Him at all.) And Christ lives within you, so even though your body will die because of sin, the Spirit gives you life because you have been made right with God. The Spirit of God, who raised Jesus from the dead, lives in you. And just as God raised Christ Jesus from the dead, He will give life to your mortal bodies by this same Spirit living within you."

- Romans 8:9-11

The heart keeps the body alive. From the heart, blood flows, carrying life, strength, and nourishment to every part of us. This is true in our physical bodies, and it is just as true in our spiritual ones.

In nature, the heart is the body's powerful pump. It sends oxygen and nutrients to every cell while removing what harms. If the heart stops, the body begins to shut down. Systems fail. Life fades.

In the Kingdom of God, the same truth stands: the heart keeps the body alive. God's heart keeps God's body alive. From His heart, His blood flows—throughout His creation, throughout His children, throughout His churches.

Jesus is the heartbeat of God. His blood is what flows through us, washing us, covering us, renewing us, and sustaining us. It is His life flowing through us that keeps us spiritually alive. Without it, spiritual systems begin to shut down until Spiritual death becomes imminent.

When our own heart feels broken beyond repair, we need to remember that His life, His blood, carry nutrients of restoration and renewal to us and protect us against future toxins.

God often hides His truths in Creation, and one of the clearest pictures of His sustaining heart is found in a simple wildflower: milkweed. Milkweed doesn't just grow; it keeps others alive the same way the heart keeps the body alive, and the same way God keeps us alive.

Monarch butterflies cannot survive without it. Hundreds of species depend on it for food, shelter, or reproduction. Its nectar feeds the weak when nothing else is blooming. Its toxins even become a shield for vulnerable caterpillars, protecting them from predators. It thrives in overlooked places and becomes a refuge for the fragile.

Milkweed Is not a separate illustration; it is nature preaching the same sermon:

Life flows outward from a single source. Strength radiates from one rooted place, and protection is given to the vulnerable through what it carries.

Milkweed is a living parable of God's heart. Just as milkweed sustains an entire ecosystem, and just as the heart sustains the body, God's heart sustains His people.

Milkweed becomes a covering, a protector, a life-source… just like Jesus. It mirrors the heart of God: A heart that nourishes. A heart that shields. A heart that sustains. A heart that keeps the body alive.

Milkweed doesn't stand beside the message; it *is* the message in Creation. It is the heartbeat of God written in the wild:

Life flows from the heart. Life flows from Him.

God, thank You for being the heart that keeps us alive. Let Your life flow through every place in us that feels weak, weary, or broken. Cover us, nourish us, and shield us the way You sustain all Creation. Teach us to rest in Your heartbeat and trust the life You are breathing into us today.

In Jesus' Name, Amen.

Your Notes

Day 22: Forward From The Ashes

"Lot reached the village just as the sun was rising over the horizon. Then the Lord rained down fire and burning sulfur from the sky on Sodom and Gomorrah. He utterly destroyed them, along with the other cities and villages of the plain, wiping out all the people and every bit of vegetation. But Lot's wife looked back as she was following behind him, and she turned into a pillar of salt."

- Genesis 19:23-26

Fireweed is one of the clearest pictures in Creation of how God calls us to move forward and not look back. When a wildfire tears through a forest and leaves nothing but ashes, fireweed is the first plant to rise. It doesn't wait for the ground to be perfect or for the environment to improve; it steps into destruction and begins the work of restoration right there.

Just like fireweed, God doesn't wait for the ground of our lives to be perfect before He begins healing us. He walks us through the destruction, planting new seeds for the future, causing something beautiful to bloom even among the ashes of what once was.

"He gives beauty for ashes…" - Isaiah 61:3

Fireweed doesn't just survive devastation; it restores what was damaged. Its roots stabilize the soil, prevent erosion, and prepare the ground for new life to return. We can do the same when we trust God to lead us out of the past. A believer who follows God forward becomes like fireweed—rebuilding what was broken instead of returning to what was lost. Don't look back.

We see this truth in the story of Lot's wife. God was leading Lot and his family out of a city destined for destruction, a city that was spiritually dead long before it turned to ash. But Lot's wife couldn't let go. Maybe she looked back because of old friendships or memories of when the city wasn't corrupt. We don't know her reasons, but we do know this: In Genesis 19:17, God's messengers warned them clearly: 'Do not look back.' And in Genesis 19:26, Lot's wife did look back—and she became a pillar of salt. God told them not to look back.Obedience to God must be greater than our feelings, our memories, and our desire to understand everything. Looking back cost her everything, not because God was cruel, but because she clung to what God was trying to deliver her from.

The same is true for us.

We don't need others to validate our hurt in order to heal from it. We need to surrender that hurt to Jesus and ask the Holy Spirit to deliver us… and He will. Sometimes, we think healing requires us to revisit the past, but it doesn't. Healing comes when we look up, not back.

"I look up to the mountains; does my help come from there? My help comes from the Lord, who made heaven and earth! He will not let you stumble; the One who watches over you will not slumber." - Psalm 121:1–3

Our help comes from the Lord. Our healing comes from the Lord. Our future comes from the Lord. The past does not dictate our future, so why look back at it? To hit the target God has set before us, our eyes must stay *on* the target. If we're looking backward, we will never hit what God is calling us toward.

Look to Jesus. Let go. Be healed in His name.

Just as fireweed signals the end of a season—marking transition and change—God does the same with us. He shows us when it's time to move on. If we refuse to listen, even if our bodies don't turn into a pillar of salt or stone, our hearts can… and that is far worse.

So, look forward. Look up. Remember where your help comes from. Don't give up. And don't look back.

A prayer for the day

Jesus, lead me forward. Help me release what's behind me and trust You with what's ahead. Plant new life in every place that once felt burned or broken, and let Your Spirit guide my steps into the future You've prepared. Keep my eyes on You, my help and my healer.

In Jesus' Name, Amen.

Your Notes

Day 23: Return to Your Tents

"Go and tell them, 'Return to your tents.' But you stand here with me so I can give you all my commands, decrees, and regulations. You must teach them to the people so they can obey them in the land I am giving them as their possession.

"So, Moses told the people, 'You must be careful to obey all the commands of the Lord your God, following his instructions in every detail. Stay on the path that the Lord your God has commanded you to follow. Then you will live long and prosperous lives in the land you are about to enter and occupy."
- Deuteronomy 5:30-33

Columbine is a wildflower that teaches us something profound about the way God leads His people. Even though its seeds can travel, most fall right back beneath the parent plant. Columbine naturally returns to the place where it first bloomed, the place where its roots were meant to grow deeper.

Sometimes, God asks us to do the same. Even though He calls us not to look back, there are seasons when He tells us to return to our tents—to go back to the last place He spoke, the last instruction He gave, the last ground where He planted us. Not to return to bondage or old patterns, but to the camp of obedience—a place of rest, reflection, and waiting.

There are seasons when the voice of God feels distant or silent, in good seasons and in hard ones. I've learned that His silence doesn't mean He is gone. It often means He is working on something in our future, preparing what we cannot yet see. In those quiet seasons, the Holy Spirit whispers, "Until you hear from God on what to do next, go back and keep doing the last thing He told you."

That's the tent—a place of shelter in the wilderness. A place where the Holy Spirit rests around you, surrounds you, and covers you while you wait for the Father to share the next step.

Just like Columbine blooms in rocky, unlikely places, God makes beauty even in the places that feel impossible. When we return to the last instruction He gave us, He often brings deeper healing, clearer vision, and fresh revelation—the things we need before stepping into the promises He is quietly preparing for our future.

We want growth to happen quickly. Sometimes, it does. But, most of the time, it doesn't. That's not failure; that's formation. With God, slow seasons produce slow and steady growth, the kind He builds to last.

The tent is not a punishment; it's protection. It's preparation. It's the place where roots deepen, faith strengthens, and identity settles. His plan is never for us to stay in our tents forever, but the tent keeps us safe in the wilderness until it's time to move into new territory and new promises. The lessons we learn in the tent become the very wisdom that carries us into the future He has prepared.

So, if God feels quiet, return to your tent. Return to the last thing He said. Return to the place where your roots can grow deeper. He is not done speaking; He is preparing you to hear. When the time comes, He will call you forward. But, until then, rest. Wait. Trust. Let Him grow you in the quiet.

A prayer for the day

Father, bring my heart back to the place where You last spoke. Settle me in the tent of Your presence, where I can rest, listen, and be held while You prepare what's ahead. Teach me not to fear the quiet seasons but to trust that You are working in the unseen. Deepen my roots where You've planted me and steady my spirit as I wait for Your next instruction. Surround me with Your peace, cover me with Your Spirit, and keep my eyes fixed on You. Lead me forward in Your timing and let every lesson in this season prepare me for the promises You've already written over my life.

In Jesus' Name, Amen.

Your Notes

Day 24: Speak to the Rock

"Moses and Aaron turned away from the people and went to the entrance of the Tabernacle, where they fell face down on the ground. Then the glorious presence of the Lord appeared to them, and the Lord said to Moses, 'You and Aaron must take the staff and assemble the entire community. As the people watch, speak to the rock over there, and it will pour out its water. You will provide enough water from the rock to satisfy the whole community and their livestock.' So Moses did as he was told. He took the staff from the place where it was kept before the Lord. Then he and Aaron summoned the people to come and gather at the rock. 'Listen, you rebels!' he shouted. 'Must we bring you water from this rock?' Then Moses raised his hand and struck the rock twice with the staff, and water gushed out. So the entire community and their livestock drank their fill. But the Lord said to Moses and Aaron, 'Because you did not trust me enough to demonstrate my holiness to the people of Israel, you will not lead them into the land I am giving them.' This place was known as the waters of Meribah (which means *arguing*) because there the people of Israel argued with the Lord, and there he demonstrated His holiness among them."

- Numbers 20:6-13

Harebell wildflowers look delicate, but they carry a strength that defies their appearance. They grow in places most plants would never survive—cliffs, rocky soil, windswept mountains, and harsh elevations. They bend without breaking, sway without snapping, and bloom where the ground is hard and the conditions are unforgiving. And, yet, they don't just survive in those places; they thrive.

Harebells teach us something about the way God calls His people to live. They don't settle for shallow soil or easy ground. They root themselves in the hard places because they are designed to reach for something higher. They grow for the promise of the bloom, not just the provision of the soil beneath them.

This is where the story of Moses striking the rock speaks loudly. God gave Moses a clear instruction, "Speak to the rock." But Moses struck it instead. It was obedience mixed with disobedience—action without trust, effort without surrender. Moses relied on his own strength instead of God's word. Yet, even then, God still provided water for His people. His faithfulness didn't fail even though Moses did.

But here's the sobering truth The generation that saw God's provision never stepped into the fulfillment of His promise. They saw water from the rock, manna from heaven, and guidance by cloud and fire, but they never stepped into the land God had prepared for them. Provision sustained them, but promise was meant to transform them.

Provision is a blessing, but Promise is the vision. Harebells don't bloom just because the soil provides for them; they bloom because they are reaching for something beyond the ground—they are reaching for the light, the height, the purpose they were created for. They grow in rocky places because they are made for more than survival.

So are we. We don't want to be people who only live off God's provision—the daily water, the daily manna, the temporary relief. We want to be people who trust Him enough to follow His voice into the fullness of His promise.

Provision keeps you alive; Promise gives you destiny.

Moses's moment teaches us that partial obedience can still bring provision, but it can cost us the promise. God will always take care of His people, but He invites us into something deeper: trust, surrender, and faith that follows His voice exactly as He speaks it.

Like the harebell, we are called to root ourselves in the hard places, to trust God in the rocky seasons, and to grow toward the vision He has spoken, not settling for what simply keeps us alive, but reaching for what brings us into the fullness of His promise.

Let us learn from Moses. Let us learn from the wilderness generation. Let us learn from the harebell. Provision is good; Promise is better. Obedience is the bridge between the two.

May we be people who don't just survive on what God provides, but step boldly into what God has promised.

Lord, make my heart like the harebell—delicate in appearance yet anchored with a strength that only comes from You. Teach me to root myself in the hard places, to bend without breaking, and to grow toward Your light even when the ground beneath me feels rocky. I don't want to live only on Your provision; I want to walk in Your promise. Strengthen my faith so I don't rely on my own ideas but trust Your voice fully. Keep my heart obedient, steady, and surrendered, like a flower rooted in hard places yet reaching for the light.

Forgive me for the moments, like Moses, when I've acted out of effort instead of trust. Thank You for Your faithfulness that remains even when mine falters. Lead me beyond survival and into the fullness of Your calling. Let nothing in me settle for less than the fullness of Your will. Help me follow Your voice completely so I can step boldly into everything You've spoken.

In Jesus' Name, Amen.

Your Notes

Day 25: We Must Not Forget

"Then Pilate had Jesus flogged with a lead-tipped whip. The soldiers wove a crown of thorns and put it on his head, and they put a purple robe on him. 'Hail! King of the Jews!' they mocked, as they slapped him across the face.

"Pilate went outside again and said to the people, 'I am going to bring him out to you now but understand clearly that I find him not guilty.' Then Jesus came out wearing the crown of thorns and the purple robe. And Pilate said, 'Look, here is the man!'

"When they saw him, the leading priests and Temple guards began shouting, 'Crucify him! Crucify him!'

"'Take him yourselves and crucify him,' Pilate said. 'I find him not guilty.'"

- John 19:1-6

Forget-me-nots are small, gentle, and easily overlooked. They bloom quietly, without demanding attention, yet they carry a name that echoes through generations: *Remember me.*

They open slowly, bloom faithfully, and return year after year; even after they die, their seeds fall into the soil so they can rise again. They are a living reminder of love that endures, loyalty that doesn't fade, and truth that refuses to be forgotten. In this way, the forget-me-not reflects Jesus Himself. Because Jesus—the One who came to save, heal, and redeem—stood before His own people and was forgotten. Not forgotten in memory, but forgotten in identity. They saw Him, but they did not behold Him. They recognized His face, but not His Glory. They heard His voice, but not His divinity.

Pilate declared he found no fault in Him, yet the very people Jesus came to love cried out, "Crucify Him."

What a tragic moment in Scripture—the Messiah standing before the ones He formed, the ones He fed, the ones He healed, and they turned their backs on Him. They were blinded by systems, by religious leaders, by their own expectations of what they thought God should do.

They believed they already knew the Torah. They believed they already knew God's plan. They believed the Messiah would come as a warrior to destroy their enemies—not as a Lamb to be slain for their sins. Before Jesus met the cross, Humanity declared Him to be just a man. Half of who He was. Half of His identity. Half of His Glory.

Even His own disciple denied Him three times. Even those closest to Him struggled to see Him clearly. Oh, the human heart, how easily it fails us. How quickly it forms opinions about God instead of receiving revelation from God. How easily it becomes familiar with Jesus, the man, while forgetting Jesus, the Messiah.

Forget-me-nots bloom as both a warning and a promise: do not forget who He truly is.

Because when we behold Him as only a man, we crucify Him with our flesh—our pride, our opinions, our assumptions, our self-made interpretations of Scripture—but when we behold Him as God, He crucifies our flesh instead. He becomes the One who transforms us, purifies us, and leads us into truth.

There were nights I held my Bible tight because it felt like the closest thing to hugging Jesus Himself. His Word became my safety blanket, my anchor, my breath. Testimonies can encourage us, but it is His Word that holds us together. His voice. His truth. His presence.

Forget-me-nots drop their seeds after they die so they can return again and again—a legacy of remembrance. Jesus, through His death and resurrection, planted a legacy that cannot be uprooted.

Just because something is finished doesn't mean it's over. It's just begun. A full release for a full future.

Death comes before resurrection. Mourning comes before new birth. The grave comes before glory.

If they persecuted Him, they will persecute you. But just as Jesus showed us, victory comes through surrender. He faced the battle, and because He yielded to the Father's will, He overcame. And, because He overcame, He now knows all things that have been accomplished. He knows what is finished. He knows what is surrendered. He knows what is rising. Forget-me-nots whisper, "Remember me;" Jesus whispers the same.

May we never forget who He truly is—not just a man, but the Messiah, the Savior, the Redeemer, and my God.

Forgot-Him-not…

A prayer for the day

Jesus, teach my heart to remember You rightly—not just as a man, but as the Messiah, the Savior, the Redeemer, and my God.

Guard me from familiarity that forgets Your Glory and awaken in me a fresh awe for who You truly are. Like the forget-me-not, let my faith bloom quietly and faithfully, returning again and again to the truth of Your Word. When my heart grows distracted, whisper, "Remember me," and draw me back to Your presence.

Forgive me for the moments I've limited You to what I expected or assumed. Purify my sight so I behold You fully—holy, powerful, and worthy of all honor. Let Your truth crucify my flesh and transform my life.

Thank You for the legacy You planted through Your death and resurrection, a legacy that cannot be uprooted. Help me carry that remembrance into every season, trusting that what feels finished is often the beginning of something new.

Jesus, may I never forget who You are or what You've done.

In Jesus' Name, Amen.

Your Notes

Day 26: Light In The Valley

"Then the Lord will create over all of Mount Zion and over those who assemble there a cloud of smoke by day and a glow of flaming fire by night; over everything the glory will be a canopy. It will be a shelter and shade from the heat of the day, and a refuge and hiding place from the storm and rain." -

Isaiah 4:5

The lily of the valley has always fascinated me—a wildflower so small and hidden, yet carrying a fragrance so sweet it fills the entire forest. It blooms low to the ground, tucked beneath shadows, surrounded by darkness, and, still, it refuses to lose its purity.

Just like the lily of the valley, purity remains purity even when shadows surround it. Darkness can hover, but it cannot corrupt what God has made holy. Even when we belong fully to Christ, there are still moments of spiritual warfare that try to interfere with God's plans—thoughts that don't sound like Him, fog that tries to settle over our clarity, and lies that convince us we are stuck, unseen, unworthy, or alone.

There was a moment when the enemy tried to pull me into that mental fog—distracting thoughts, discouraging lies, the kind that loop over and over until you start to believe them. But, in that moment, the Word of God broke through like light cracking open a dark room. I was reading Isaiah 4:5, and the scripture didn't just speak, it leapt off the page and wrapped itself around my heart. It was revelation… prophecy… the Holy Spirit breathing truth into places where lies had tried to settle.

Zion rose from the page first, not just a place, but a picture of God's Kingdom on earth, a home for wanderers, a refuge for the weary, a place where justice and righteousness flow like living water. Suddenly, I understood that when God speaks of Zion and all her assemblies, He is speaking of His Church, His people, His children—the ones who carry His name and His purity, just like the lily of the valley carries its fragrance.

Then came the cloud, the quiet, hidden presence of God that waters the thirsty and sustains life, even when we cannot see Him clearly. The cloud reminded me that God is never absent, never distant, never silent. Even when our thoughts feel loud, and even when the enemy tries to distort our vision, God is still covering, still nourishing, still near.

Then came the fire, not destructive fire, but phōs, the pure, brilliant light that breaks darkness and exposes truth. The kind of light that reveals what is real and burns away what is false. The kind of light that interrupts lies mid-sentence and reminds you who you are and *whose* you are.

And then there was the canopy—God's covering, His shelter, His protective defense stretched over His people like a shield. A place where purity is preserved. A place where the enemy's arrows fall, powerless. A place where the child of God can rest without fear.

All of it came together at once—Zion, cloud, fire, canopy—and, suddenly, the lily of the valley made sense in a way it never had before. Just like that flower, we are planted in a world where shadows exist, but we are not defined by them. We are surrounded, at times, by darkness, but we are not consumed by it. We may feel hidden, but we are never unprotected. We may hear lies, but we are held by truth. The purity God placed in us—the purity of His Spirit, His calling, His identity—cannot be touched by the enemy's voice.

The enemy isn't after your possessions; he's after your faith. He uses circumstances, thoughts, memories, and fears as weapons to try to shake what God has spoken over you.

But Isaiah 4:5 reveals the reality the enemy hopes you never see: that God Himself surrounds you. That His presence waters you. That His light guides you. That His Glory covers you. That His truth exposes every lie before it can take root. That His protection is stronger than any attack formed against you.

So, no matter what or who tries to steal your peace, no matter what thoughts rise up against the knowledge of God, no matter what fog clouds your vision, the truth remains: the Lord will bring justice and safety to you. He will provide life, and life more abundantly, the kind Jesus spoke of in John 10:10. He will be with you in every moment of your day. Even the darkness of night will be broken by the Holy Spirit, who guides us and refines us from within. He will lead you into something greater. You will be protected. His Glory will be your shelter, your defense, your covering.

You are the lily of the valley in His garden—pure, resilient, fragrant with His presence, untouched by the lies that try to surround you. The God who planted you is the God who covers you, the God who lights your path, the God who waters your soul, and the God who calls you His own.

A prayer for the day

Lord, thank You for being the God who meets me in the shadows and keeps my spirit pure even when darkness presses in. Like the lily of the valley, help me stay rooted in humility, hidden in Your presence, and fragrant with Your holiness. When the enemy whispers lies, when fog settles over my clarity, when thoughts rise that do not sound like You, break through with Your light. Let Your truth interrupt every lie mid-sentence.

Surround me with Zion—Your Kingdom, Your people, Your covering. Let Your cloud rest over me, nourishing what feels dry, reminding me that You are never distant. Let Your fire guide me, exposing what is false and illuminating the path ahead. Stretch Your canopy over my life, shielding me from every arrow, guarding the purity You placed within me.

Strengthen my faith when the enemy tries to shake it. Anchor me in the reality that You surround me, You protect me, and You speak louder than any lie. Let Your Glory be my shelter, Your presence my peace, and Your Word my light in every dark moment.

I am Yours—planted by Your hand, covered by Your Spirit, and called by Your name. Keep me resilient, steady, and fragrant with Your presence. Lead me into truth, guard me with Your Glory, and let me rest in the safety of Your love.

In Jesus' Name, Amen.

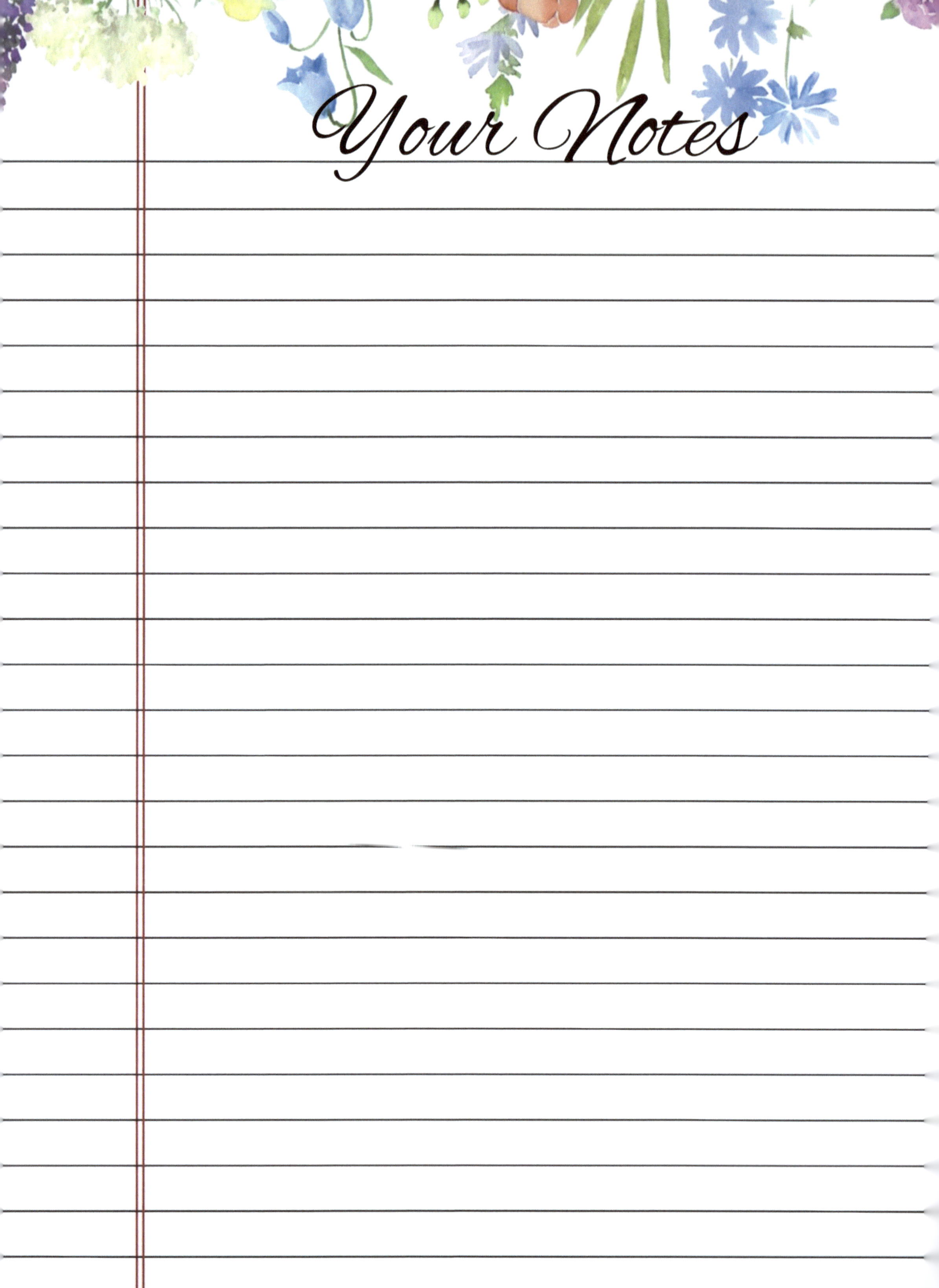

Your Notes

Day 27: Bold Blooms Of Obedience

"For if you remain silent at this time, relief and deliverance for the Jews will arise from another place, but you and your father's family will perish. And who knows but that you have come to your royal position for such a time as this?"

- Esther 4:14

Goldenrod has always reminded me of Queen Esther—not because they look alike, but because they *live* alike. Goldenrod rises in seasons when other flowers fade. It stands tall when the landscape grows weary. It blooms in the late heat, in dry places, and in the overlooked corners of Creation, bringing life to everything around it.

Isn't that exactly what God did through Esther? She didn't step into her calling in a season of ease; she stepped into it in a moment of crisis when fear was loud, destruction was near, and insecurity could have easily silenced her. Yet God placed her in the palace, not by accident, but for such a time as this. Just like goldenrod, she bloomed when others were fading, standing in courage when everything around her trembled.

Scripture makes something very clear: "For if you remain silent at this time, liberation and rescue will arise for the Jews from another place." That line shakes me every time. It reminds us that God's will is never fragile. His plans will unfold… with us or without us. But obedience is an invitation to be part of the miracle.

We can choose silence, fear, or hesitation, but why would we want to? Silence leads to prolonged battles. Hesitation leads to unnecessary pain. Disobedience delays deliverance. If Esther had stayed quiet, who knows how many lives would have been lost—including her own. But her obedience ensured safety, breakthrough, and Divine protection for an entire nation.

Goldenrod teaches the same truth. It doesn't wait for perfect conditions. It doesn't shrink back when the season shifts. It shows up boldly, bravely, and beautifully. Its boldness is not loud; it's faithful and consistent, obedient to the season God placed it in.

That's the kind of boldness God calls us into—not the boldness of volume or personality, but the boldness that grows each time we obey the voice of God. Boldness that comes from trusting Him again and again. Boldness that rises in the face of fear, stands firm in the face of destruction, and steps forward in the face of insecurity. Boldness that says, "If God placed me here, then here is where I will bloom."

You were born for such a time as this. You are not here by accident. Your life carries purpose, weight, and Divine timing. God is not surprised by your circumstances; He prepared you for them. With Him, you can be brave when fear tries to silence you, strong when destruction tries to shake you, and courageous when insecurity tries to shrink you.

So, be like Esther. Be like goldenrod. Stand tall in the season God planted you in. Be brave. Be bold. Walk in the royalty of who you truly are… a beloved child of the King.

A prayer for the day

God, thank You for placing me on this earth for such a time as this. When fear rises, make me brave. When insecurity whispers, make me steady. When the enemy tries to silence me, let Your Spirit speak louder. Cover me with Your wisdom, strengthen me with Your courage, and anchor me in obedience to Your voice. Just as You empowered Esther to stand in her moment, empower me to stand in mine. Let my life shine like goldenrod in hard seasons—bold, bright, and full of purpose—bringing life to everything around me. I trust that You are with me, You go before me, and You will accomplish Your will through my surrendered yes.

In Jesus' Name, Amen.

Your Notes

Day 28: Restoration After Ruins

"The Spirit of the Sovereign Lord is upon me, for the Lord has anointed me to bring good news to the poor. He has sent me to comfort the brokenhearted and to proclaim that captives will be released and prisoners will be freed. He has sent me to tell those who mourn that the time of the Lord's favor has come, and, with it, the day of God's anger against their enemies. To all who mourn in Israel, He will give a crown of beauty for ashes, a joyous blessing instead of mourning, festive praise instead of despair. In their righteousness, they will be like great oaks that the Lord has planted for His own glory. They will rebuild the ancient ruins, repairing cities destroyed long ago.

"They will revive them though they have been deserted for many generations. Foreigners will be your servants. They will feed your flocks and plow your fields and tend your vineyards. You will be called priests of the Lord, ministers of our God. You will feed on the treasures of the nations and boast in their riches.

"Instead of shame and dishonor, you will enjoy a double share of honor. You will possess a double portion of prosperity in your land, and everlasting joy will be yours."

- Isaiah 61:1-7

Bee Balm also known as Wild Bergamot has always struck me as another prophetic wildflower in creation. It grows in places where the land has been burned, cleared, or left barren. It rises in the very places where other plants have died. Instead of being defined by what was lost around it, Bee Balm becomes the source of life for an ecosystem. Bees and butterflies return because of it.

What looked like a wasteland becomes a nursery for transformation. What looked empty becomes essential. What looked dead becomes the birthplace of something beautiful.

And isn't that exactly how God restores us?

I've lost a lot in this life—a husband, best friends, a church family I'd once served with my whole heart. I've had people walk away not because of my sin, but because of the sins of others. I've watched purpose slip through my fingers. I've felt the sting of abandonment, the ache of confusion, and the weight of being misunderstood. I've lost relationships, stability, and what felt like my place in the body of Christ. I've lost wealth, security, and the sense of home.

But here's the truth I now know deep in my bones: we don't truly lose anything God has called us to have. People are accountable to God. Seasons shift. Circumstances change. But nothing God ordains can be stolen forever. Everything in this life is on borrowed time—even the things we love most. And yet, God restores. Not always the same things, and not always the same people, but always something better, deeper, stronger, and more aligned with His heart.

Scripture says, "The enemy has stolen… but God restores sevenfold." That means God doesn't just give back—He multiplies. He rebuilds. He redeems. He transforms loss into life the same way Bee Balm transforms burned ground into a sanctuary for returning pollinators.

Bee Balm teaches us that what looks like the end is often the beginning. That what feels like devastation can become the soil of destiny. That God can use the very places of loss to birth new purpose. Looking back now, living in the restoration of things I'd once thought were gone forever, I see the truth: God never let anything be taken from me that He wasn't planning to replace with something better.

Yes, losing people hurts—deeply. Losing dreams hurts. Losing community hurts. But we have a choice: we can let the hurt shut us down, isolate us, and convince us to never try again… or we can let gratitude soften the pain, let memories remind us of beauty, and let God lead us into healing and new beginnings.

Hurt has a strange way of pulling us closer to God. We get wounded, and He becomes the healer. We get abandoned, and He becomes the One who stays. We lose, and He becomes the One who restores. Sometimes, that cycle repeats throughout life—not because God is cruel, but because He is forming something unshakeable in us.

We are human; we will hurt others and others will hurt us—sometimes intentionally, sometimes unintentionally. But my prayer is that hurt never becomes a weapon the enemy uses to isolate you, silence you, or convince you that you are safer alone. Don't let past wounds keep you from trying a new church, building new friendships, or stepping into love again when God says it's time. People come and people go. Hurt happens—but so does healing. The enemy steals, kills, and destroys, but God restores.

You are stronger than you think. You are braver than you feel. And you will be okay—truly okay. Just wait, pray, and lean into God. He will show you the way. He always has. He always will.

And, like Bee Balm rising on top of what once had died, you will bloom again—and what grows next will carry more life than what was lost.

A prayer for the day

Lord, thank You for being the God who brings life out of barren places. Like Bee Balm growing where everything else has died, help me rise in the very places loss tried to break me. You know every wound, every abandonment, every dream that slipped through my hands—and yet, You are the One who restores, rebuilds, and multiplies what was stolen. Heal the hurt that still lingers. Guard my heart from isolation, bitterness, and fear. Soften me with gratitude, steady me with Your presence, and lead me into the new friendships, new purpose, and new beginnings You've prepared.

Be my healer when I'm wounded, my companion when I feel alone, and my restorer when life feels stripped bare. Form something unshakeable in me through every season of loss and every season of rebuilding. And, when the time is right, help me bloom again—stronger, fuller, and able to carry more life than what was lost.

In Jesus' Name, Amen.

Your Notes

Day 29: Cannot Be Uprooted

"yet Christ has now reconciled you [to God] in His physical body through death in order to present you before the Father holy and blameless and beyond reproach— [and He will do this] if you continue in the faith, well-grounded and steadfast, and not shifting away from the [confident] hope [that is a result] of the gospel that you have heard, which was proclaimed in all creation under Heaven, and of which [gospel] I, Paul, was made a minister."

- Colossians 1:22-23

Prairie dock is one of the most unmovable wildflowers in Creation. Its taproot can reach astonishing depths, so deep that, once it's established, it is nearly impossible to uproot. Storms can bend it, winds can shake it, and seasons can change around it, but prairie dock remains. Its strength isn't in what you see above the surface; its strength is hidden, anchored, rooted in a place no storm can touch.

That is exactly what a life rooted in God looks like. Everything we read in Scripture is truth—alive, active, and breathing in our world and in our hearts. God's Word is not ink on paper; it is the voice of the living God shaping us, strengthening us, and driving our roots deeper every time we read it.

We all fall short of the Glory of God, but the free gift of eternal life through Jesus is what anchors us. His grace is the soil our roots grow into. His Spirit is the water that nourishes us. His truth is the strength that makes us unmovable. Just like prairie dock, once our faith roots go deep, we become nearly impossible to uproot.

But deep roots don't grow by accident. Prairie dock takes time to establish itself… and so do we. We must choose to read our Bible, choose to pray, choose to worship, and choose to sit with God long enough for our roots to reach the depths where storms can't touch us. Becoming unmovable is not about being loud, forceful, or outwardly strong; it's about being anchored.

Anchored things don't always look powerful. Sometimes, becoming unmovable looks sturdy and strong; other times, it looks vulnerable and weak. Sometimes, it looks like standing tall; other times, it looks like falling to your knees.

In your weakness, there is power—and that power has a name. You are tough, but not because you pretend to be. You are tough because you are weak. You are vulnerable because you walk in fellowship with Him and with others who strengthen you. Your strength is not self-made; it is God-given.

Sometimes, strength is movement—pressing forward, stepping out, obeying boldly. But, sometimes, strength is stillness. Stillness is not passivity; it's surrender. It's choosing to *not* act in your own strength so you can be moved by His.

When we are still, we stop being the force that drives our lives. We stop striving, pushing, and trying to manufacture our own strength. In that stillness, we become positioned for transformation. Because when an outside force presses upon something still, it moves. Our outside force is Christ.

When we allow Him to be the One who moves us, we move in His strength, His timing, His direction. This is what it means to be unmovable: not that *we* never move, but that only *God* moves us. We still our flesh so the Spirit can lead. We quiet our fear so His courage can rise. We surrender our will so His can be done. We root ourselves in truth so lies cannot shake us.

Prairie dock teaches us that the deepest strength is hidden. The strongest faith is anchored. The most unmovable life is the one rooted in Christ. That, when your roots grow deep, you will stand through storms, endure seasons, remain unshaken, and move only when moved by Him.

Jesus, anchor my heart in You. Grow my roots deep into Your truth until nothing in this world can shake me. Let Your Word come alive in me—active, breathing, shaping, strengthening—so my faith becomes steady and unmovable. Teach me to be still so I can be moved by Your Spirit and not by my flesh. In my weakness, show Your power. In my vulnerability, reveal Your strength. Make me sturdy, grounded, and rooted in Your love. Lead me, steady me, and hold me in every season. I surrender my motion, my striving, and my fear, and I ask You to be the One who moves me. Establish me in Your presence and let my life stand firm in You.

In Jesus' Name, Amen.

Your Notes

Day 30: The Final Petal of Praise

"Nothing Can Separate Us from God's Love, What shall we say about such wonderful things as these? If God is *for* us, who can ever be *against* us? Since he did not spare even His own Son, but gave Him up for us all, won't He also give us everything else? Who dares accuse us whom God has chosen for His own? No one—for God Himself has given us right standing with Himself. Who then will condemn us? No one—for Christ Jesus died for us and was raised to life for us, and he is sitting in the place of honor at God's right hand, pleading for us. Can anything ever separate us from Christ's love? Does it mean he no longer loves us if we have trouble or calamity, or are persecuted, or hungry, or destitute, or in danger, or threatened with death? (As the Scriptures say, "For your sake we are killed every day; we are being slaughtered like sheep." No, despite all these things, overwhelming victory is ours through Christ, who loved us. And I am convinced that nothing can ever separate us from God's love. Neither death nor life, neither angels nor demons, neither our fears for today nor our worries about tomorrow—not even the powers of hell can separate us from God's love. No power in the sky above or in the earth below—indeed, nothing in all creation will ever be able to separate us from the love of God that is revealed in Christ Jesus our Lord."

- Romans 8:31-39

Asters have always amazed me. They are the last wildflowers to bloom, waiting until late summer and even into fall to reveal their beauty. When everything else has faded, asters burst into color—purples, blues, pinks, whites—like tiny starbursts across the fields. Their very name means "star," reminding us that, even in the final stretch of a season, God can still bring light, beauty, and purpose.

Asters bloom when the world thinks the blooming season is over… and, honestly, so do we.

As I reflect on this final devotional, I am in awe of God—His goodness, His timing, and His purposes that stretch far beyond our human minds and wildest expectations. When God first whispered to me to write this book, I laughed. Me? Write a book? I didn't feel smart enough. The enemy loved to remind me that I graduated with my GED—as if that disqualified me from being used by God.

But shame and human limitations have no hold on God's plans.

When I walked through abuse, divorce, loss, abandonment, unbelief, and confusion, I kept a journal. I didn't know then that I was actually writing these seeds that would bloom later. When it came time to write this devotional, imagine my shock when I realized I already had thirty devotionals from those painful seasons. God had been preparing me long before I knew I needed preparation.

Then came the title: Waiting With the Wildflowers—words the Holy Spirit spoke to me. I initially thought it was an album, but He said, "No, it's a book." My plan was simple: copy-and-paste the devotionals I had already written. But God said, "I want you to tie each devotional to my Creation—to the wildflowers."

I had no idea how to do that. Some connections felt impossible to my human mind. But obedience opened a door I hadn't even known existed.

As I studied wildflowers—their growth, resilience, and symbolism—I realized something breathtaking: the Gospel is whispered through Creation. God's fingerprints are everywhere. His story is written in petals, roots, seasons, and blooms. And every time I obeyed, He revealed more.

Never let your thoughts, the words of others, or the lies of the enemy stop you from doing something that feels scary or something you feel unqualified for. When God says, "Would you do this?"—do it. Faith is stepping out on nothing and landing on a foundation you couldn't see before.

God rarely calls the qualified. But He always qualifies the called. When we partner with Him, nothing is impossible—even if we feel like late bloomers, even if we think we've missed it. Asters remind us that blooming late is still *blooming*. Sometimes, it's the most beautiful bloom of all.

Scripture says, "He who began a good work in you will carry it on to completion until the day of Christ Jesus."
- Philippians 1:6

God finishes what He starts. He completes what He begins. He brings to fullness what He plants.

I pray this devotional has strengthened your faith, encouraged you to keep going, and inspired you with the Gospel woven through the petals of each wildflower—just as it has inspired me while writing it. Our stories carry more meaning than we can comprehend. Our lives hold more purpose than we can measure.

Trust God. Walk with Him. And watch the testimonies grow—like asters blooming long after the world expects the season to be over. Because, with God, it's never too late to bloom.

A prayer for the day

Lord, I lift up every person who feels behind, overlooked, unqualified, or unsure of their place in Your story. Just as asters bloom long after the world thinks the season is over, remind them that, with You, it is never too late to shine, to grow, or to begin again.

Speak to those who doubt their worth. Silence the lies that tell them they are not enough. Break the power of shame, insecurity, and every voice that tries to disqualify what You have already called. Let them feel Your delight, Your choosing, and Your confidence in their lives.

For those walking through seasons of loss, confusion, or waiting, show them that the seeds planted in pain can bloom into purpose. Reveal how You have been preparing them in hidden places, shaping them through every trial, and writing testimonies long before they ever recognized them.

Give them courage to obey when You whisper, "Would you do this?" Strengthen their faith to step out even when the path feels impossible. Remind them that You never call the qualified; You qualify the called. And that, when they partner with You, nothing is out of reach.

Lord, finish the good work You began in them. Bring to completion every promise, every calling, every dream You planted. Let their lives burst into color in Your perfect timing—bright, beautiful, and full of purpose.

May they trust You deeply, walk with You boldly, and bloom In ways that surprise even them. Because, with You, it is never too late to bloom.

In Jesus' Name, Amen.

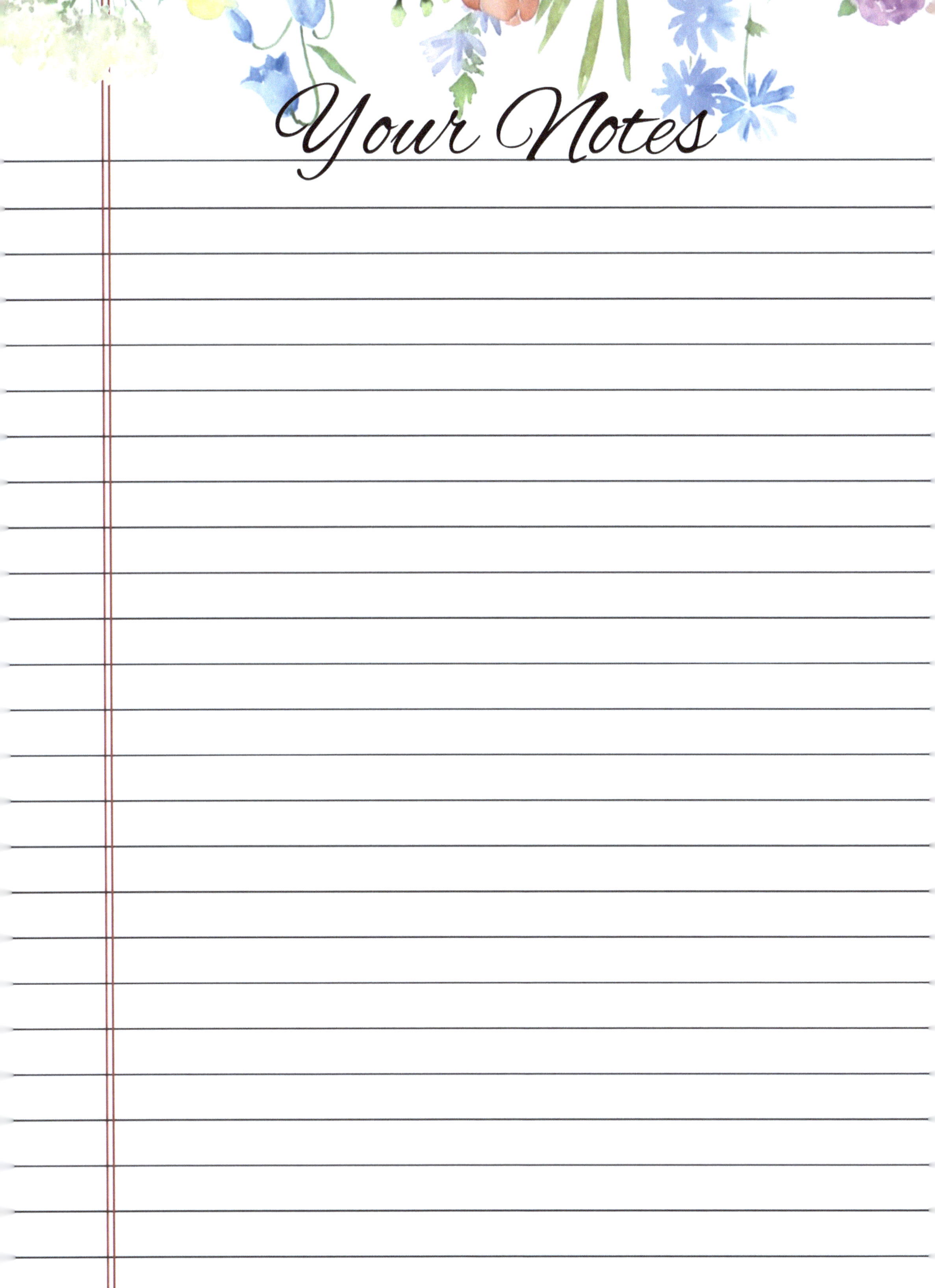

Your Notes

Acknowledgments

This devotional was birthed out of prayer, surrender, and the steady faithfulness of God. Every page reflects His goodness, His patience, and His gentle way of turning our stories into testimonies. I am humbled that He would trust me with these words, and my deepest prayer is that they draw you closer to His heart.

To my mother, Sharon, thank you for encouraging me long before I ever believed I had something worth saying. Your strength, your resilience, and your unwavering belief in what God placed inside me have been a constant source of courage. You have always reminded me that healing is possible and that our stories matter.

To my husband, Forrest, thank you for reminding me daily of the goodness of God. You see me the way He does, even on the days I struggle to see it myself. Thank you for speaking life over me, for telling me, "God wouldn't ask you to write this if He didn't already know you could," and for standing beside me with a faith that steadies my own. Your love has been a reflection of Christ's heart toward me.

To the friends who stayed when life grew heavy and the road grew long—thank you. You didn't let fear, distance, or uncertainty destroy what God called sisterhood, friendship, and family. You held space for me, prayed for me, and stood firm when everything felt fragile. I love you more than words, and you know who you are.

To my pastors and leaders throughout the years, with a special shout out to Pastor Chad & Jade Spencer, and Pastor Nathan & Heather Emmelhainz, your spiritual guidance, wisdom, and encouragement have shaped so much of who I am today. Thank you for teaching me how to hear God's voice, how to walk in truth, and how to trust Him with every part of my story. Your leadership has left a lasting imprint on my life and my faith.

To every reader who opens this devotional, thank you for allowing these words into your heart and your quiet moments with God. May each page draw you deeper into His presence, remind you of His nearness, and awaken hope in places you thought were silent.

Above all, to Jesus, my Savior, my Healer, my constant companion. Every word belongs to You. Thank You for turning my broken places into wells of living water and for proving, again and again, that nothing surrendered to You is ever wasted.

References

- The Holy Bible (Translations used, ESV, NLT, NIV, AMP)

- Strong's Concordance

- https://www.britannica.com/plant/wildflower

- https://mywildflowers.com/index.asp

- https://uswildflowers.com/wfquery.php

- https://www.amazingfactshome.com/fun-facts-about-flowers/

About the Author

Jessica Cunningham encountered Jesus in the midst of an abusive marriage, where His relentless love led her to salvation and a transformed life. Her journey since has been marked by both valleys and victories, shaping a deep resilience and an unwavering devotion to God.

She has served as a worship leader, youth leader, and Outreach Lead Coordinator on church staff. Jessica holds a degree in Christian Studies and carries a genuine passion for the Kingdom of God—especially for persevering through life's pain while pressing forward with Him. Throughout her story, she has witnessed marriage restored, removed, and completely renewed. She has lived as a working mother, a single mother, and a stay-at-home mother.

Jessica's heart beats for worship as a lifestyle, not just a position. She loves encouraging the Church and those around her with the hope of the gospel. Her prayer for this book is that God uses it to anchor your heart closer to Him, bring peace in the middle of uncertainty, and reveal the depth of His goodness—even when life doesn't feel good.